BY HUMAN ART ™

The Hummingbird Series Volume 3
Artist Drawn Spiritually Balancing Coloring Book

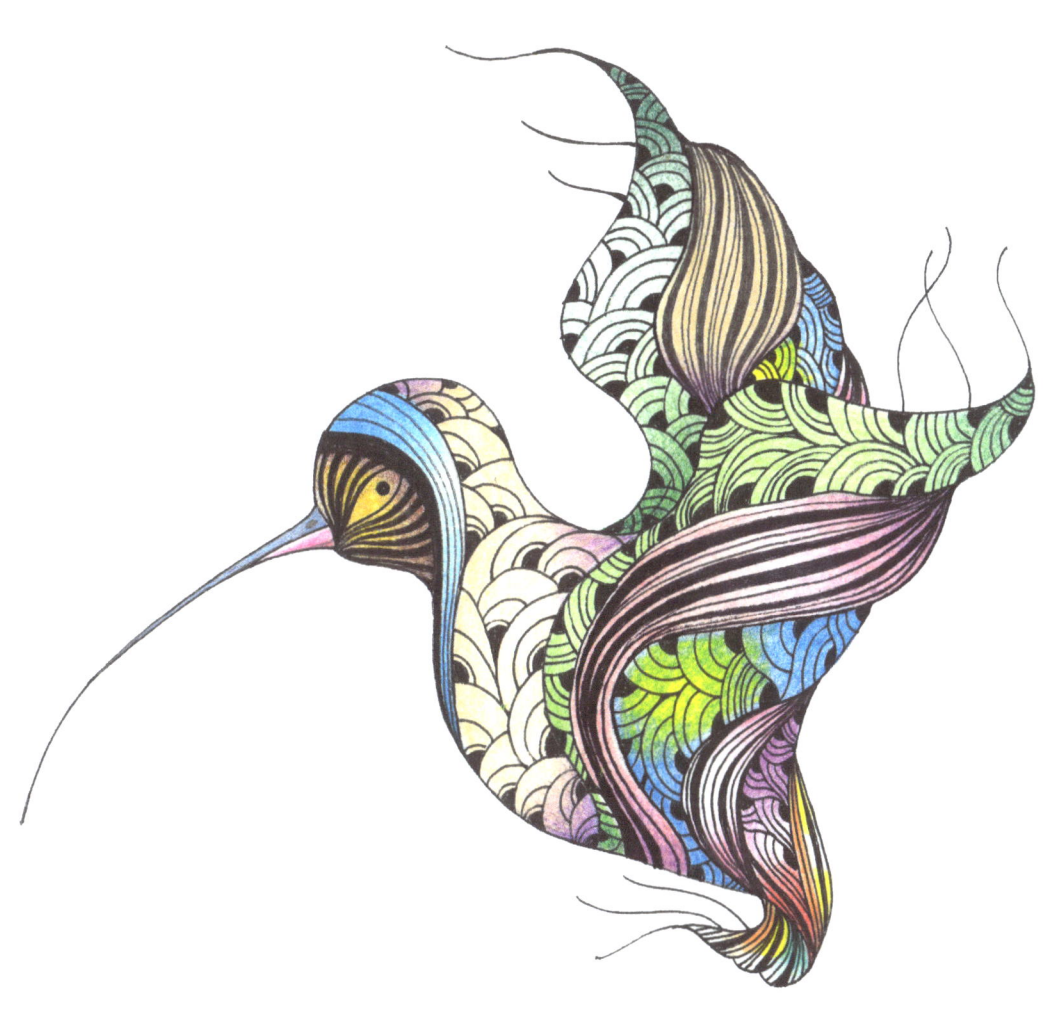

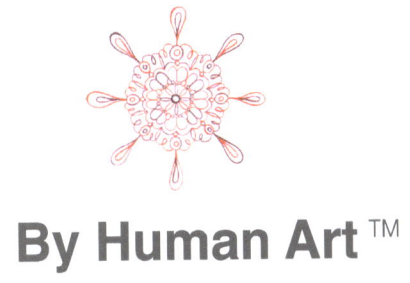

By Human Art ™

Copyright © 2017 By Human Art ™
Artwork by Maurice Howard listed below

Image 1
Image 2
Image 3
Image 4
Image 5
Image 6
Image 7
Image 8
Image 9
Image 10
Image 11
Image 12
Image 13
Image 14
Image 15
Image 16
Image 17
Image 18
Image 19
Image 20
Image 21

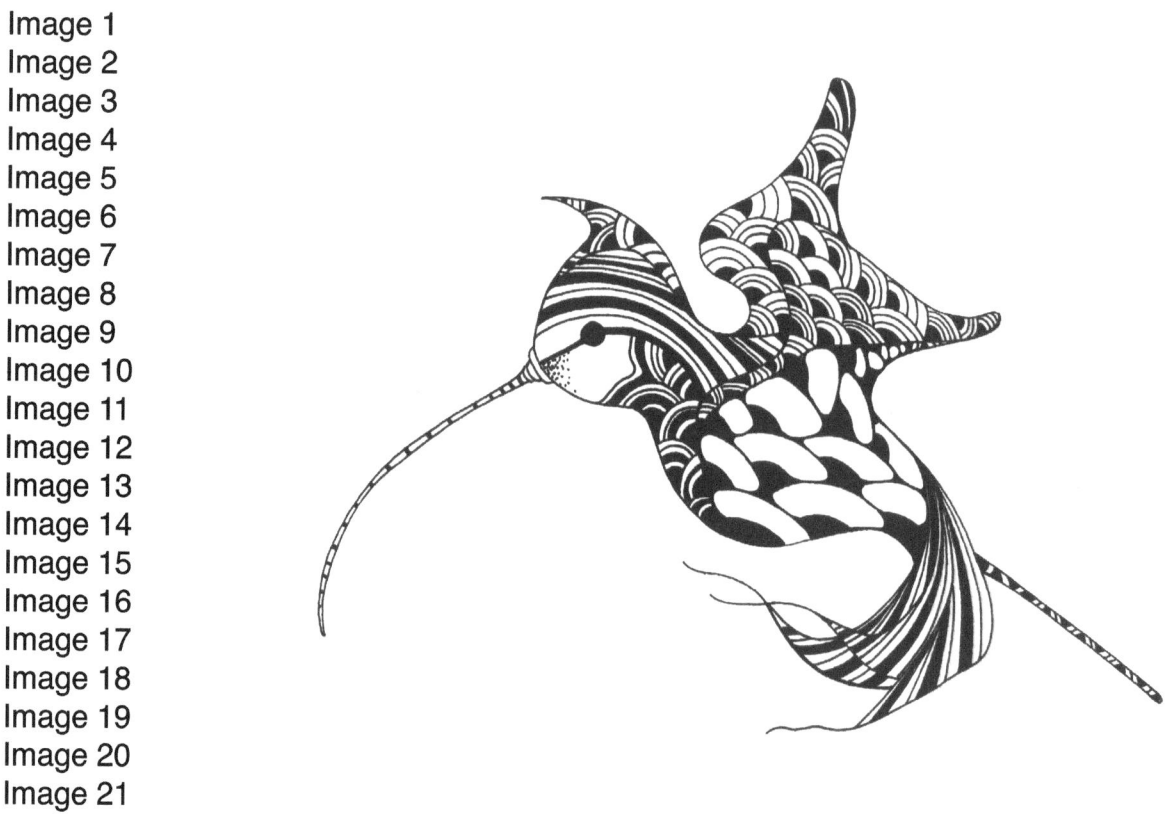

Find out which images are available on our website: ByHumanArt.com

All rights reserved. No part of this book may be reproduced in any manner without the express written consent of the publisher, except in the case of brief excerpts in critical reviews or articles. All inquires should be addressed to By Human Art P.O. Box 35294, Los Angeles, California 90035

By Human Art books may be purchased in bulk at special discounts for sales promotion, corporation gifts, fund-raising, or educational purposes.

For details, contact By Human Art
P.O. Box 35294, Los Angeles, California 90035
Library of Congress Cataloging-in-Publication Data is available on file

Illustrations and Coloring by Maurice Howard
Author and Art Director by Craig M. Davis
Graphic modifications by Rafael Rodriguez

Print ISBN – 13: 978-0692818299 (By Human Art)

Printed in the United States

CRAIG M DAVIS
Author & Art Director

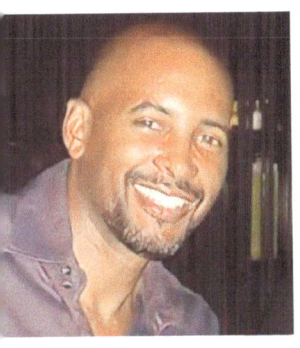

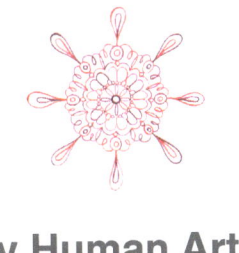

By Human Art ™
Artist Page

MAURICE HOWARD
Illustrations and Coloring

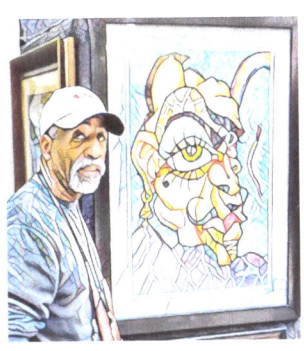

My writing career began on the Fresh Prince of Bel-Air followed by The Jamie Foxx Show. In 2005 my marketing talents from Morehouse College were called upon to consult in the personal care industry, the same industry my father participated in as the co-founder of Pro-Line Hair Company in 1970. I choose to follow in my father's footsteps and helped to author two new brands launching in 2017, JoshuaOriginals.com and Buddha-Butter.com.

Here's how I got involved in the Adult coloring book industry, in September of 2016, a good friend, Gi'ana Garel, called me and told me all about the therapeutic aspects of Adult coloring books. I was interested and began researching the market, only to witness endless computer generated images filling up the majority of the coloring books on the market.

I discovered Maurice's hummingbirds while looking for a birthday gift for my mother. I told the manager I wanted to meet him and two weeks later we met in October of 2016. I convinced Maurice to extend his collection into a five volume series, and he agreed to turn his beautifully colored Hummingbirds into black and white images also. I became a fan of work once again after learning that his technique of coloring puts you in a meditative state, I knew it was the right time to release these hidden masterpieces to the world.

Howard's method of coloring using interlocking figure eights are named "The Infinity Stroke." This technique provides a unique approach to filling empty space, which quiets the mind and sharpens concentration. I'm proud to be the author and art director for all five volumes of Maurice Howard's Hummingbirds collection.

Born in Waco, Texas, adventures began early for Maurice Howard, whose father's career in the military allowed him the opportunity to travel through Europe. While residing in France, Howard remembers the museums he visited and the lasting impression the art had on his spirit.

At the age of 19, then residing in Southern California, Howard's global exposure to art inspired his desire to paint, which led to the pursuit of a degree in art illustration from Cal State Fullerton College.

Howard brings a unique perspective to all his art, with over forty-five years of experience as an artist; Maurice's career in illustration began at Hanna-Barbera Production Studio in the 1970's. Heavily influenced by African Cubism, Chinese art, and masters like Salvador Dali; Howard's diverse style infuses several captivating themes in his Hummingbird series.

Maurice's complex shading and blending of colors breaks all the rules set by standardized coloring books, which is stay inside the lines. "Life isn't that way, it's a complex integration of many colors blending together against the fabric of life," was once quoted by Howard. Within these pages we have provided you 21 beautifully colored Hummingbirds by Howard. Witness a master of color and shading inspire you to stay inside the lines, but outside the box.

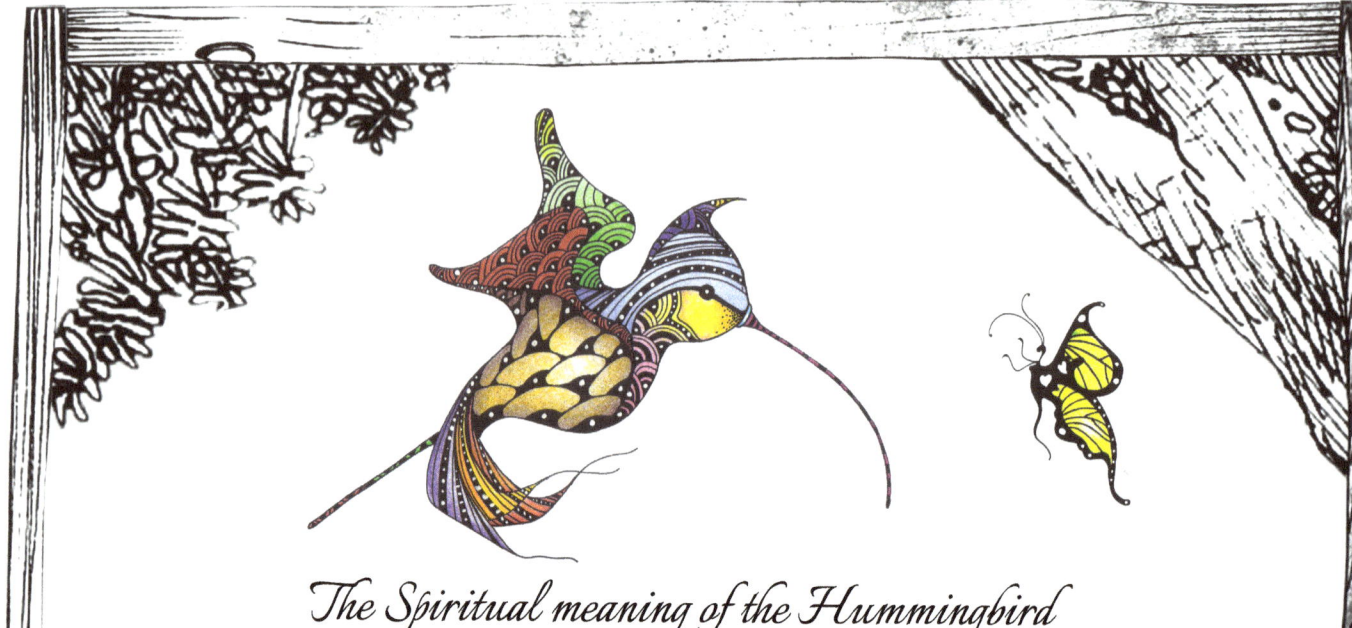

The Spiritual meaning of the Hummingbird

The Hummingbird as a spiritual animal symbolizes freedom of life and lightness of being. This ornate creature is known to behold the power of removing negativity wherever it may creep in, thus allowing the expression of love more fully in a person's life.

This fascinating bird is capable of the most amazing feats despite its small size, such as traveling great distances or being able to fly backwards. When choosing the Hummingbird as your spiritual totem, one becomes encouraged to develop their adaptability and resiliency, while keeping a playful and optimistic outlook on life.

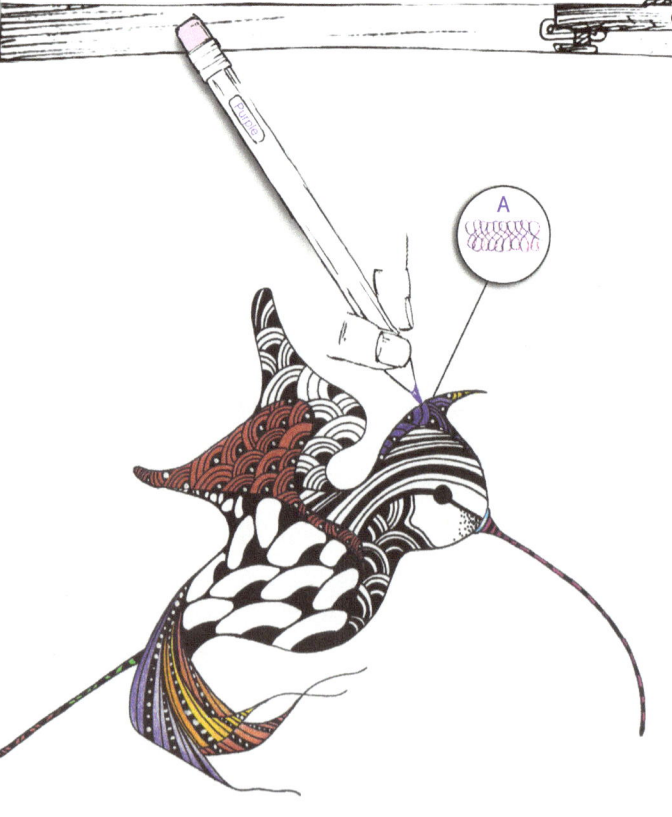

Infinity Stroke ™

The unique coloring process we call "The Infinity Stroke" allows you to tap into limitless color combinations and pattern choices within each intricate hummingbird design.

Normal coloring techniques are linear, therefore making it difficult to control color concentrations. "The Infinity Stroke" technique allows wonderful illuminating effects when overlapping light colors within dark looping colors.

This spiritually balancing technique connects those who use it to the continuous flow of the Universe. The midpoint of the infinity symbol interlocks two poles, representing balance and the endless possibilities. Experience coloring like it's your first time when using "The Infinity Stroke." Feel the flow.

"The Infinity Stroke" is illustrated in diagram A.

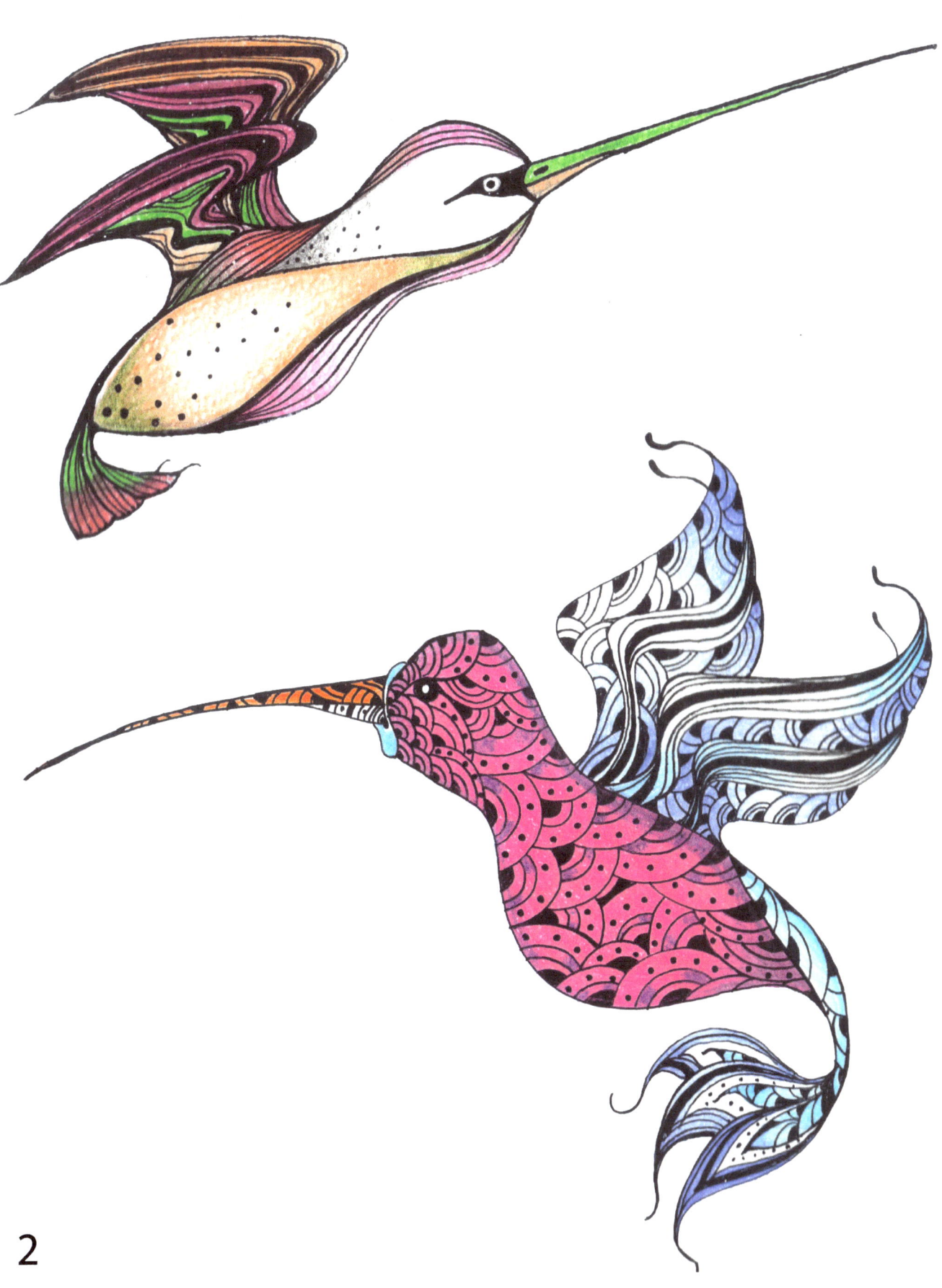

1

2

3

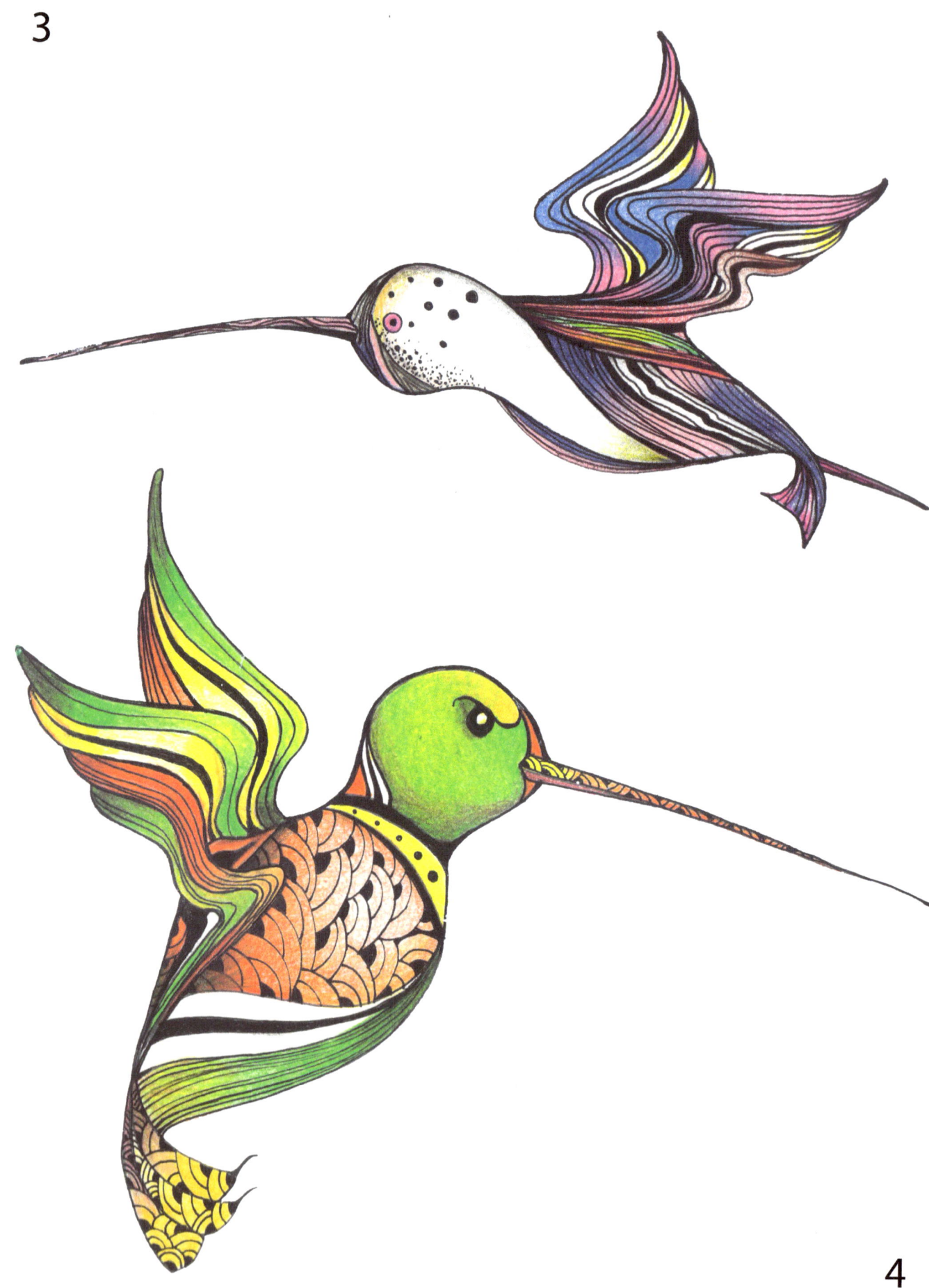

4

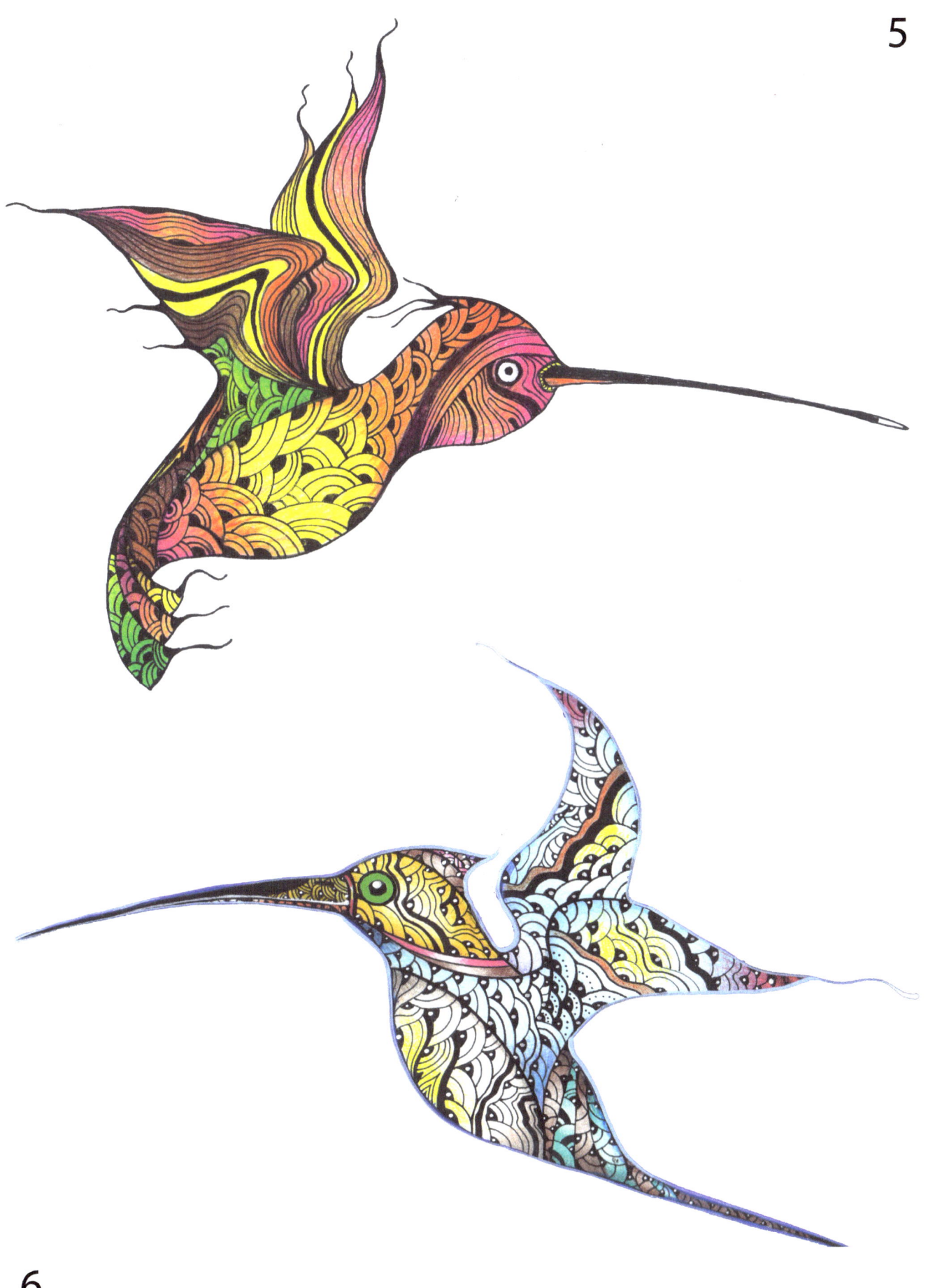

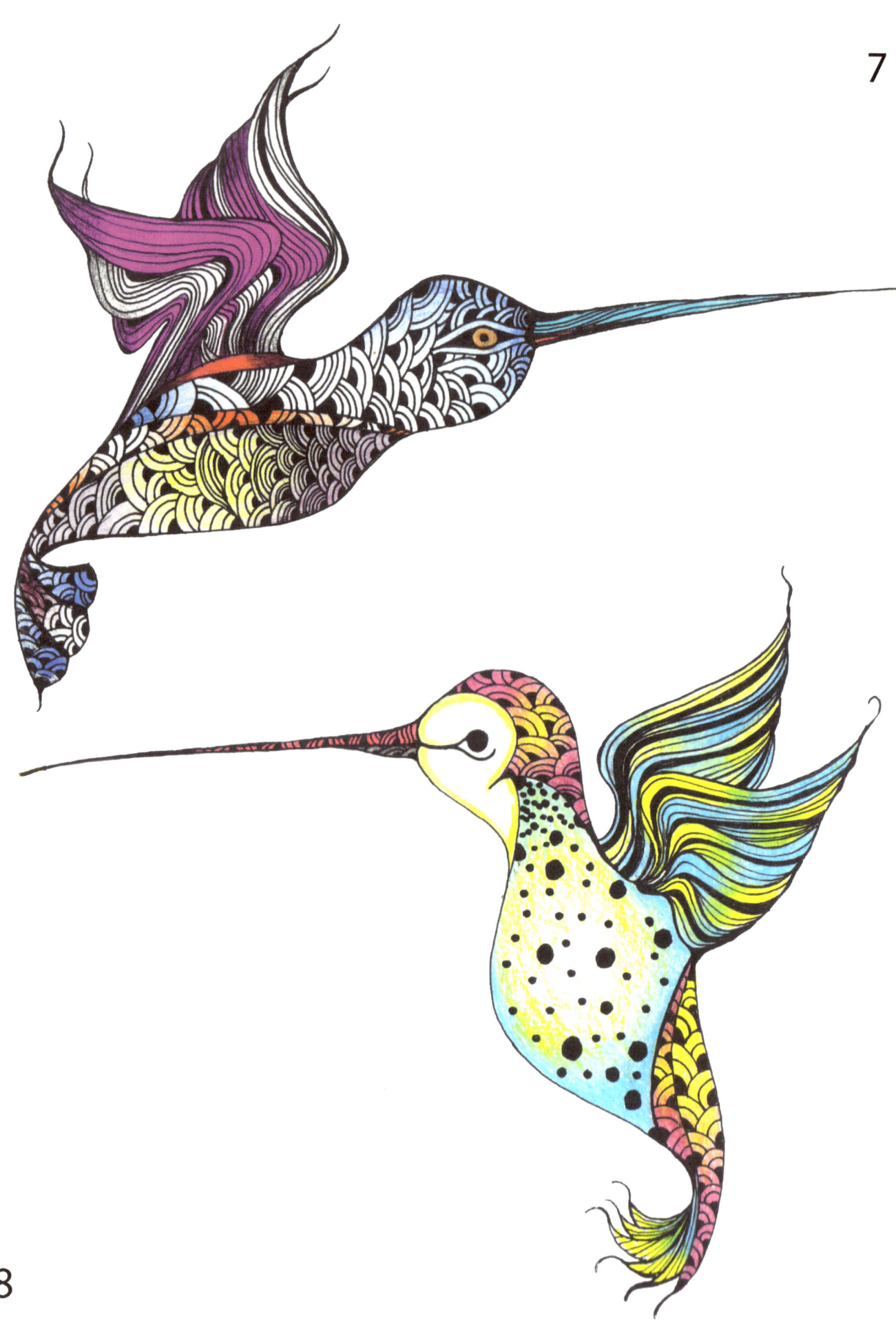

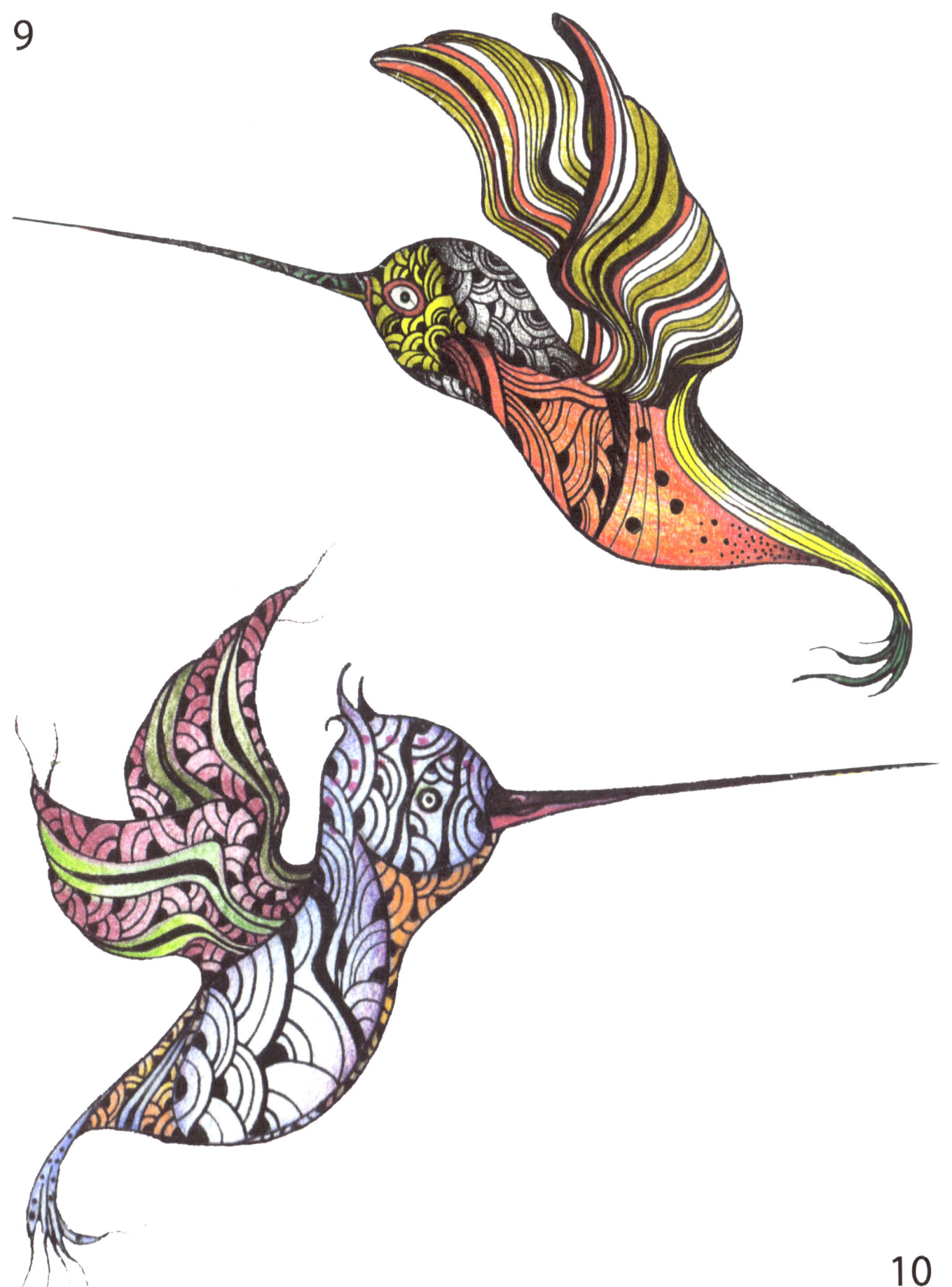

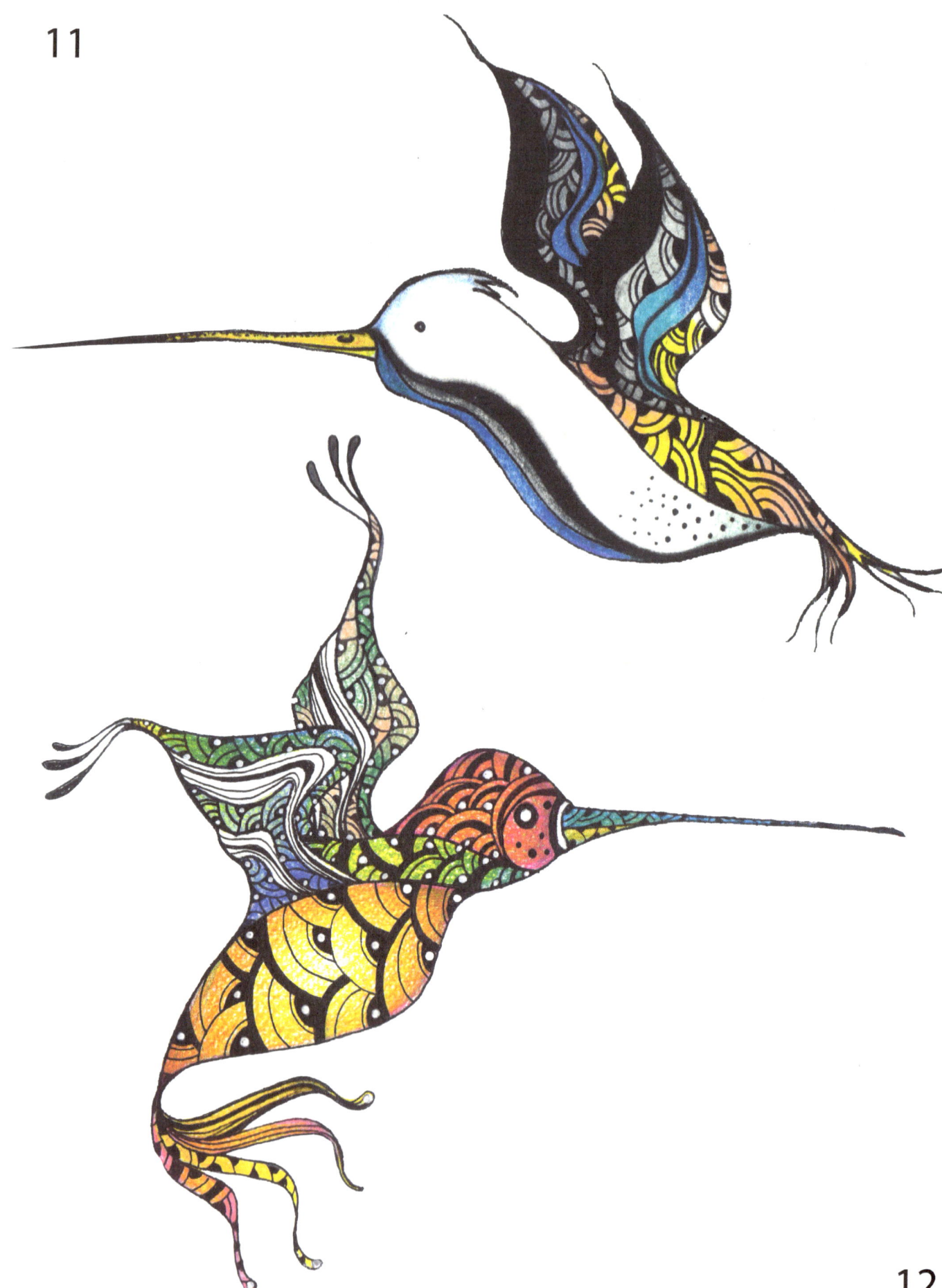

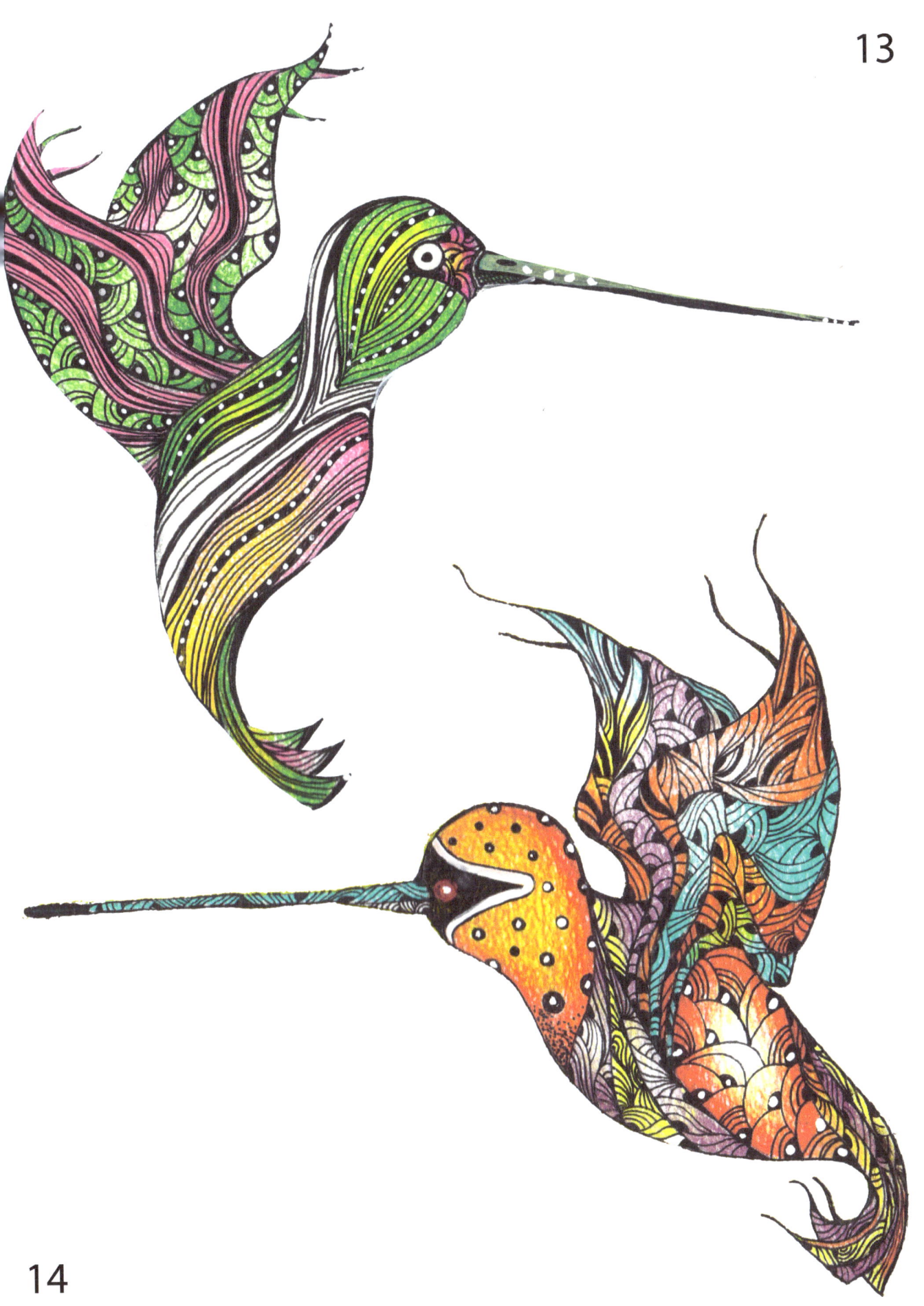

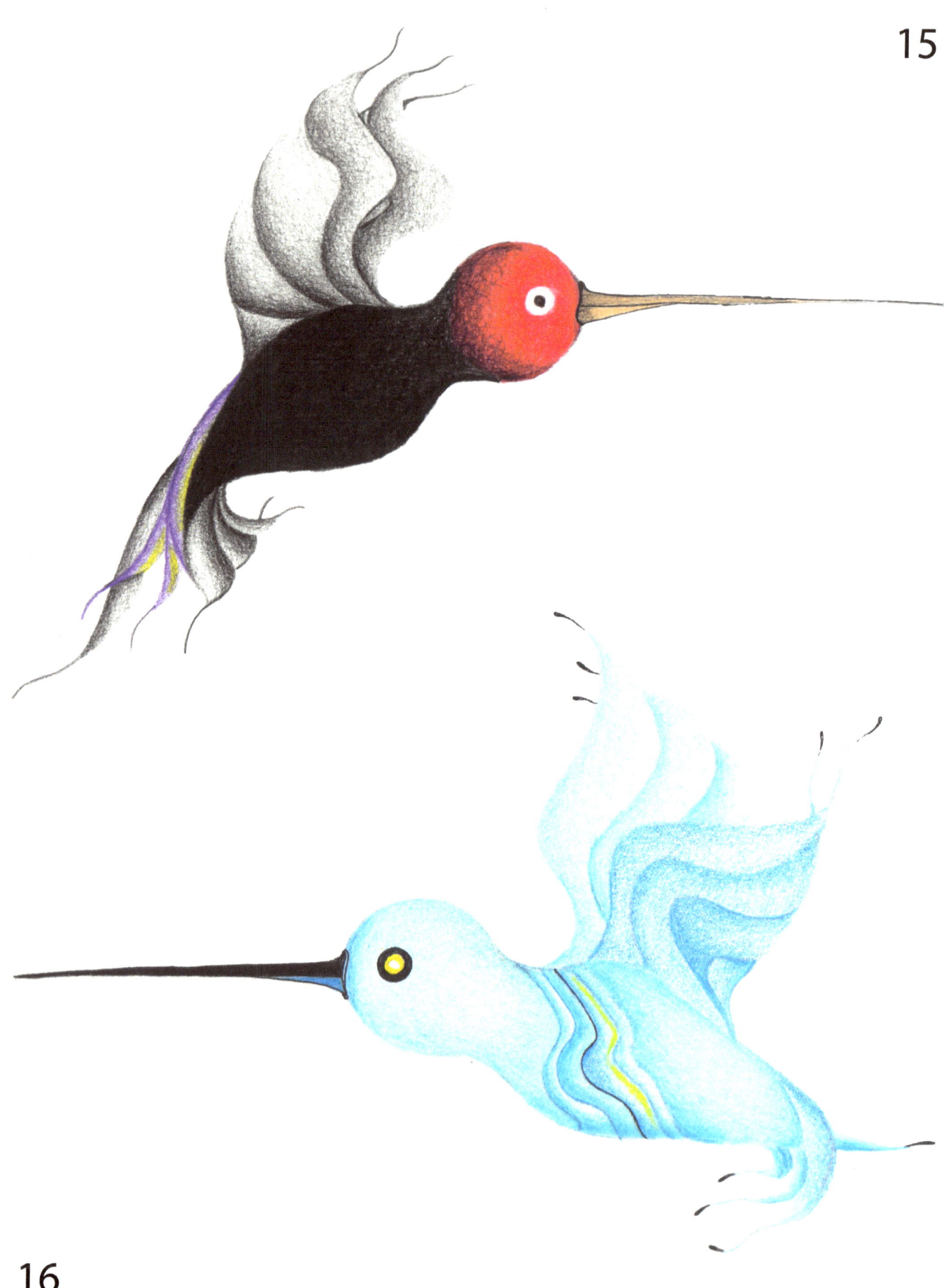

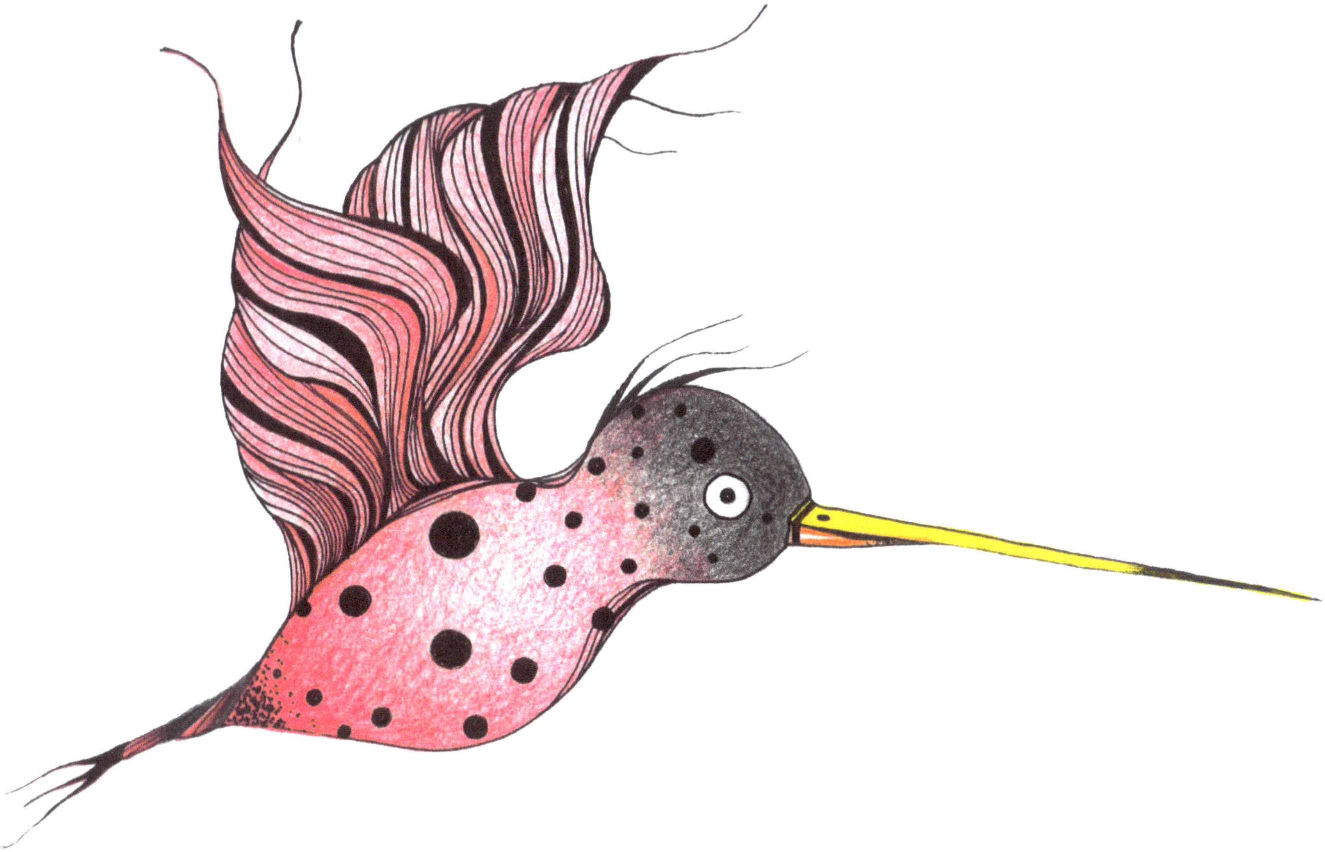

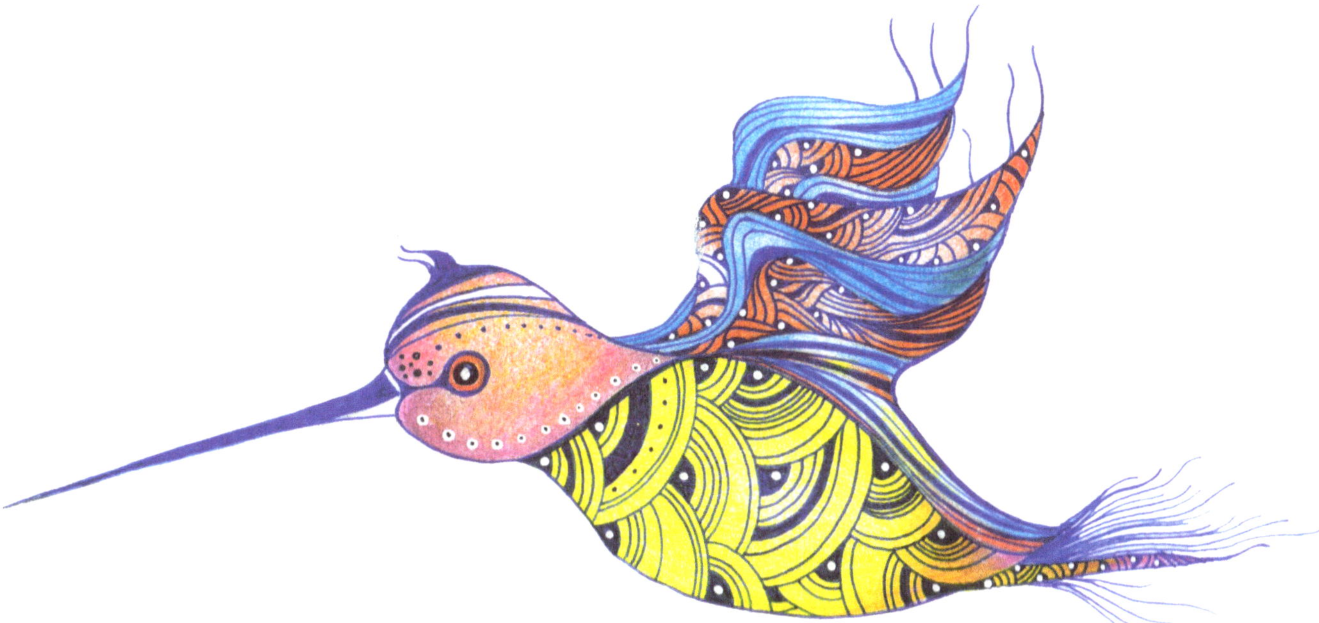

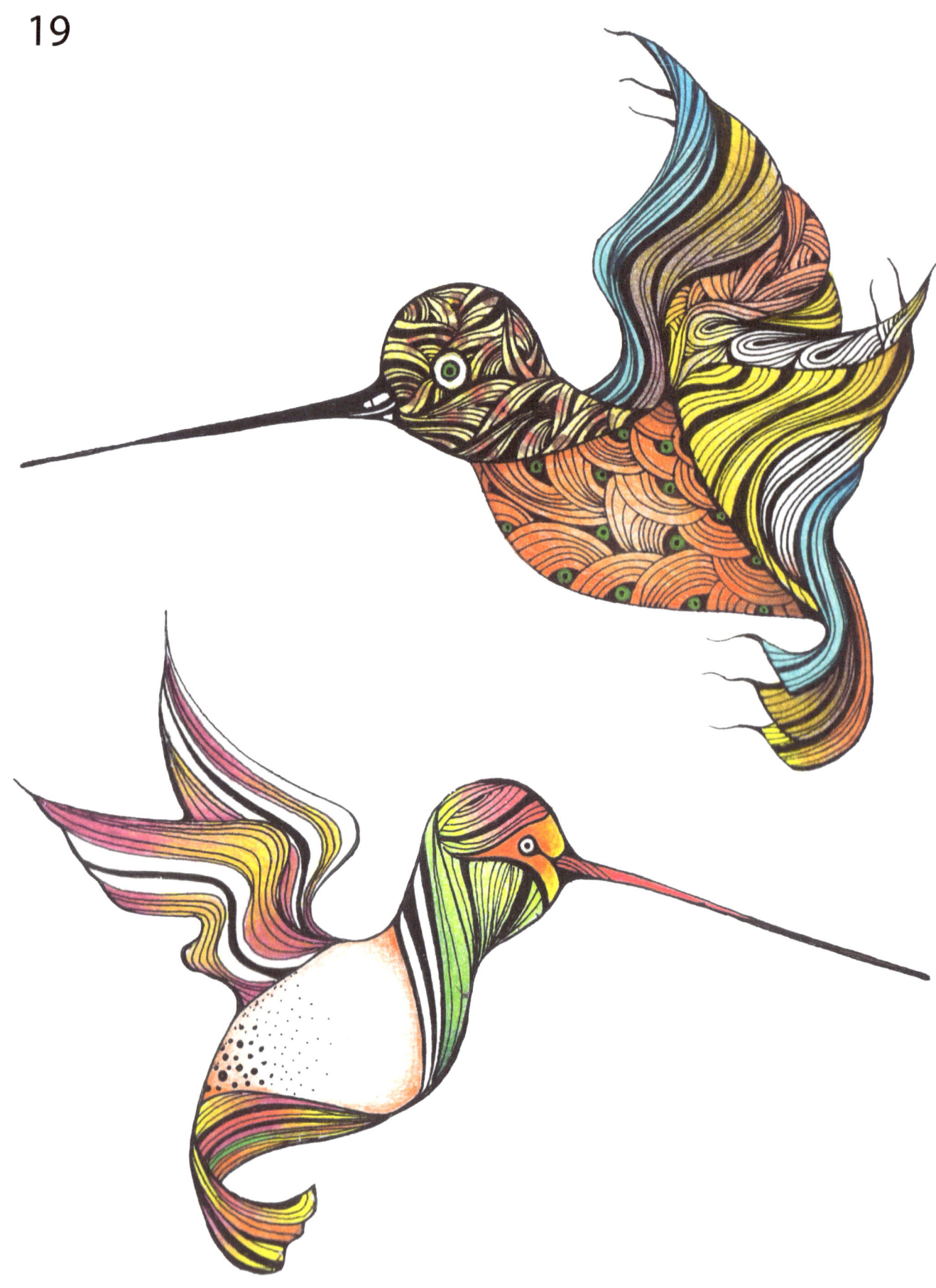

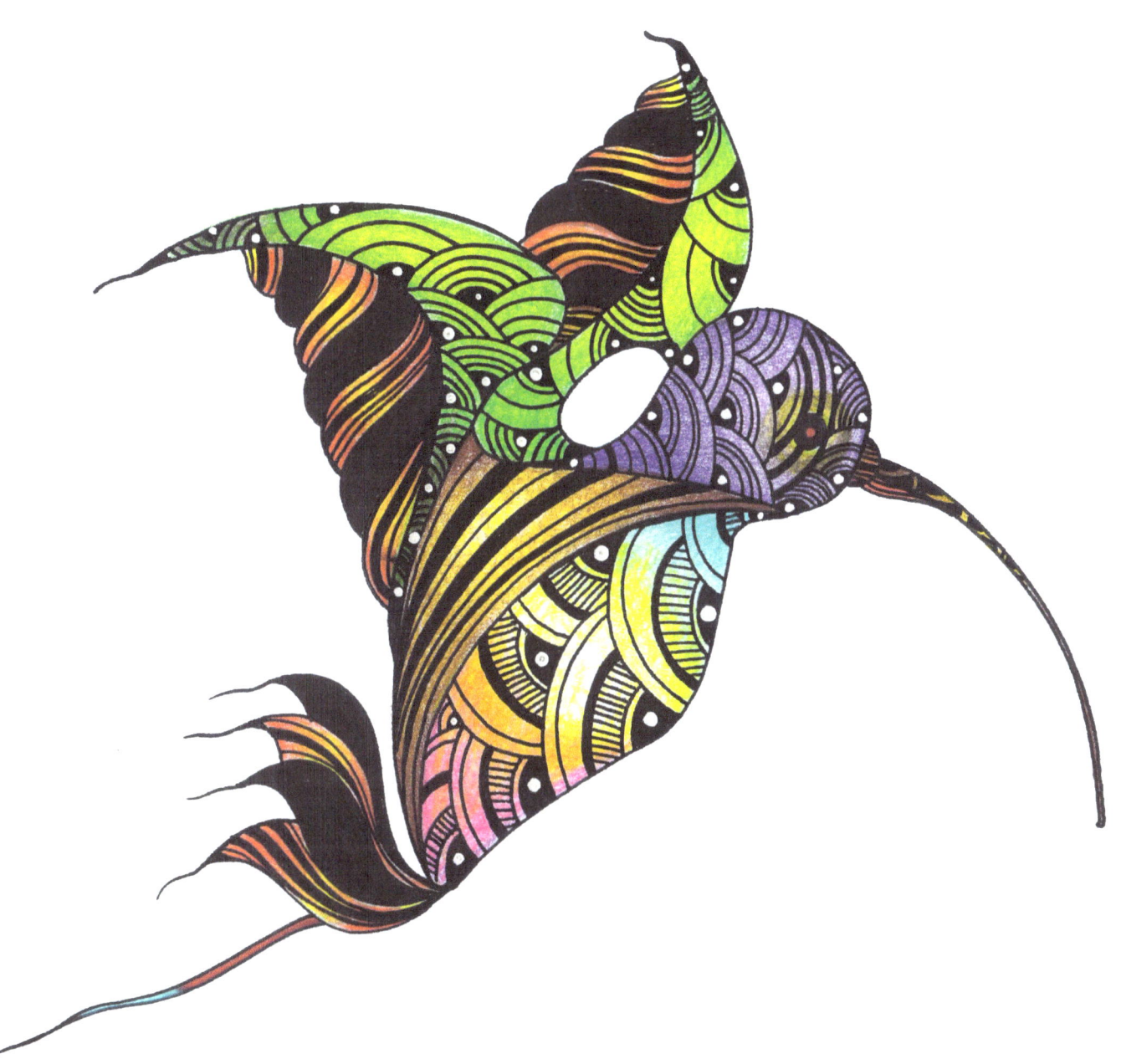

Get your colored pencils ready,
it's time to accept the challenge and create your own masterpieces.
It's okay to take a look back at some of Howard's shading techniques;
we can only become inspired from the greats.

Now turn on some of your favorite relaxing music
and look forward to hours of meditative exploration.

The key to implementing *The Infinity Stroke* is a light touch of
continuous figure eights when coloring and overlapping colors.
Now you are prepared to experience the next level in coloring.
Ready, set, go and remember to feel the flow.

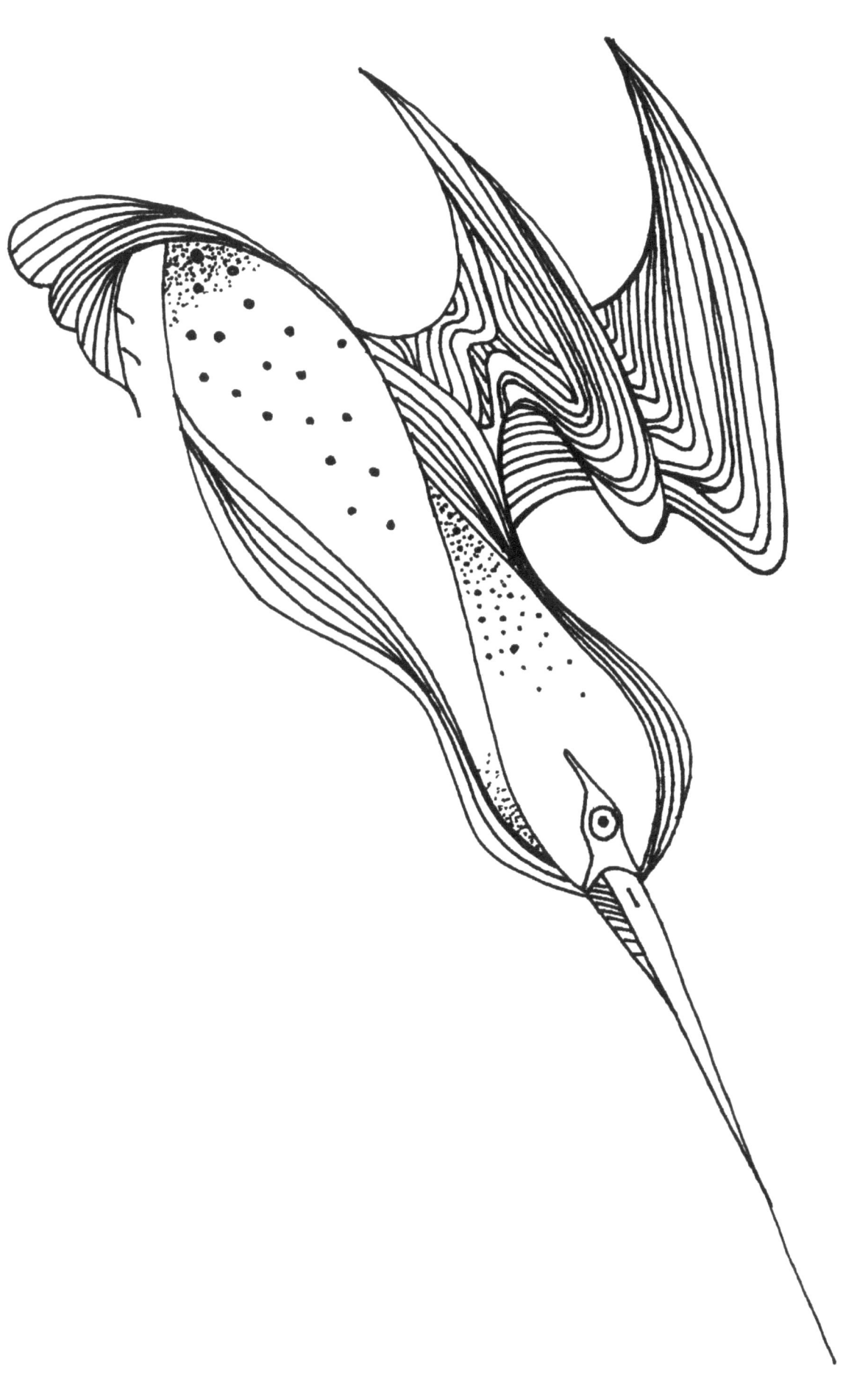

← ——————— 1

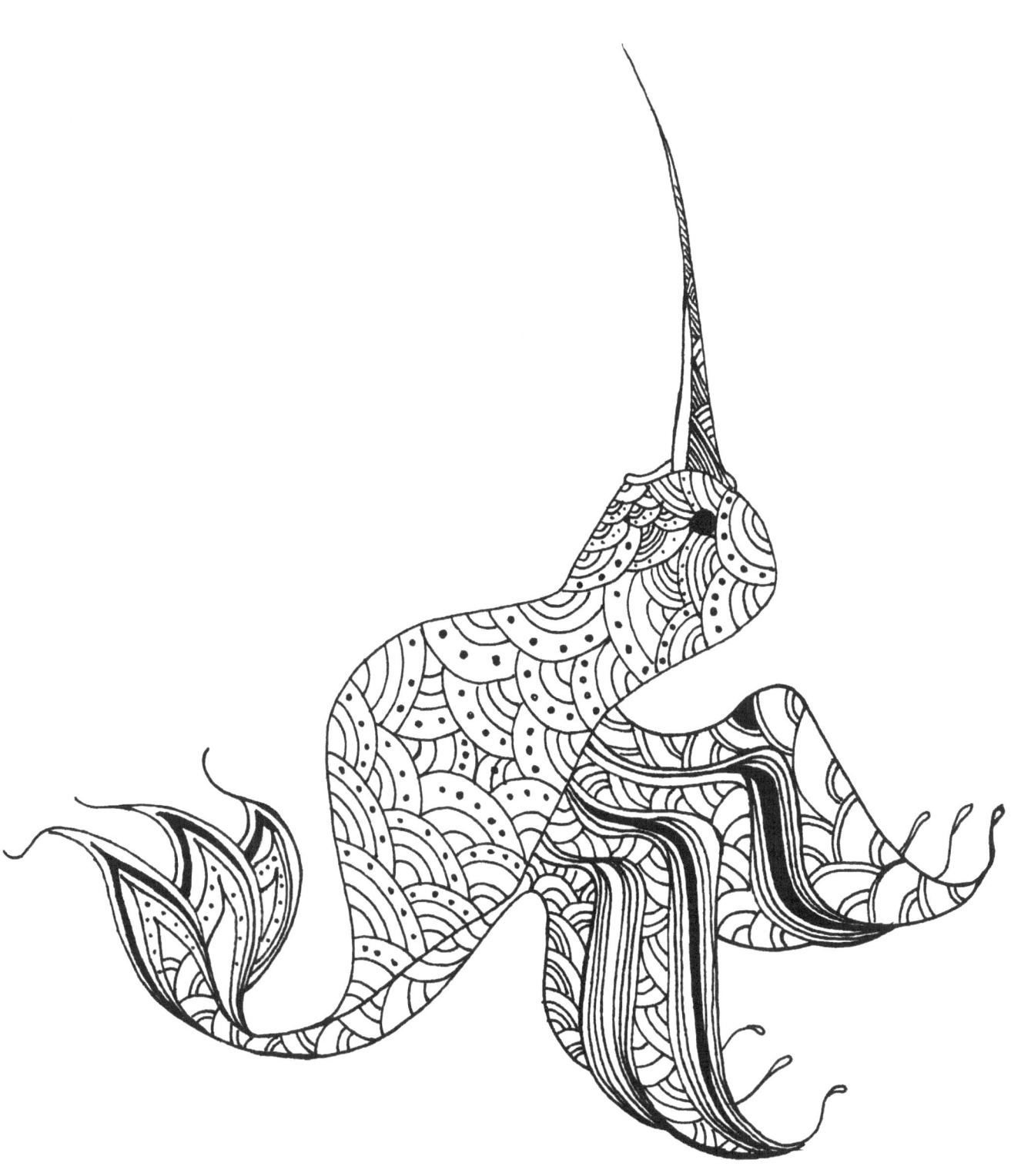

2

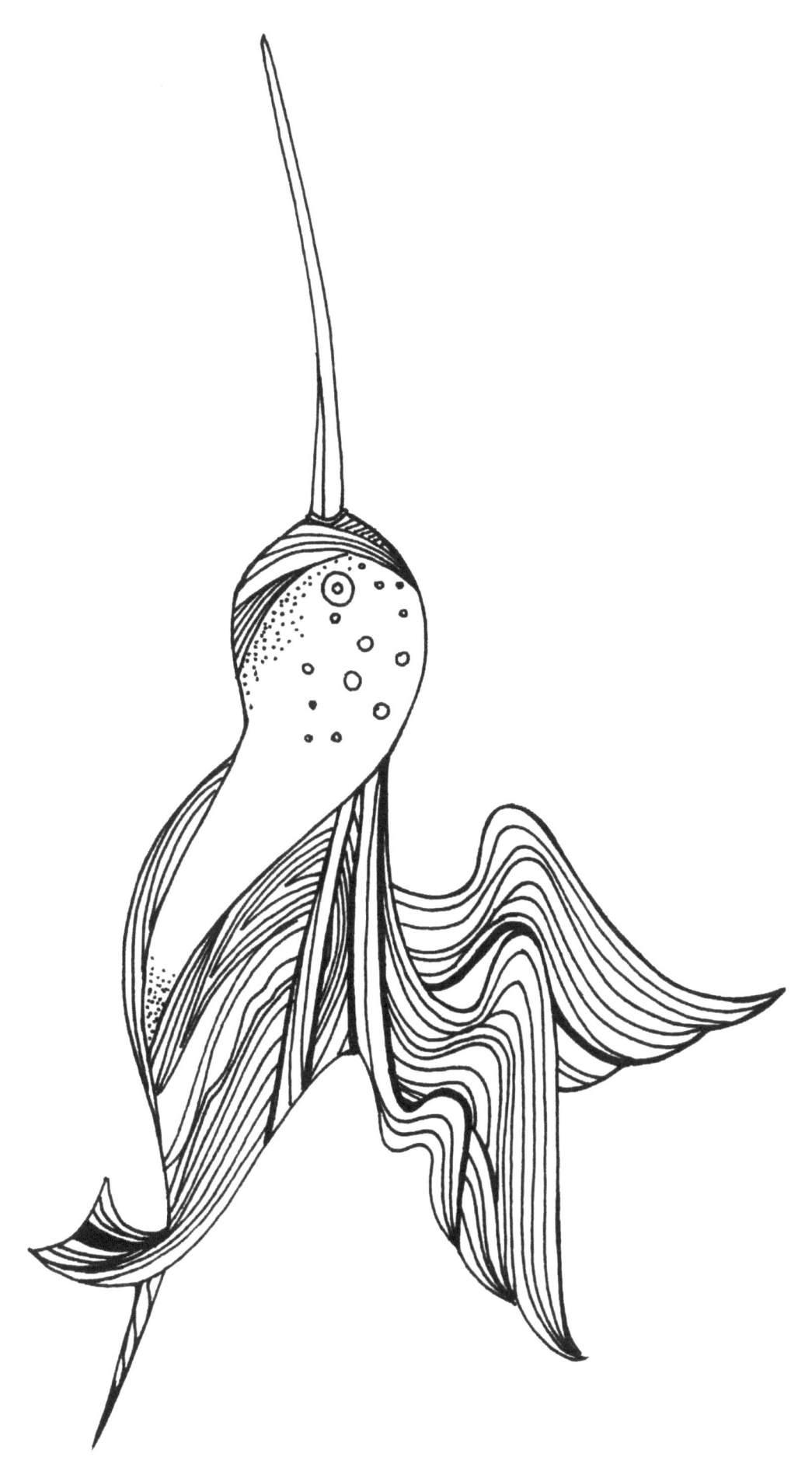

←——————— 3

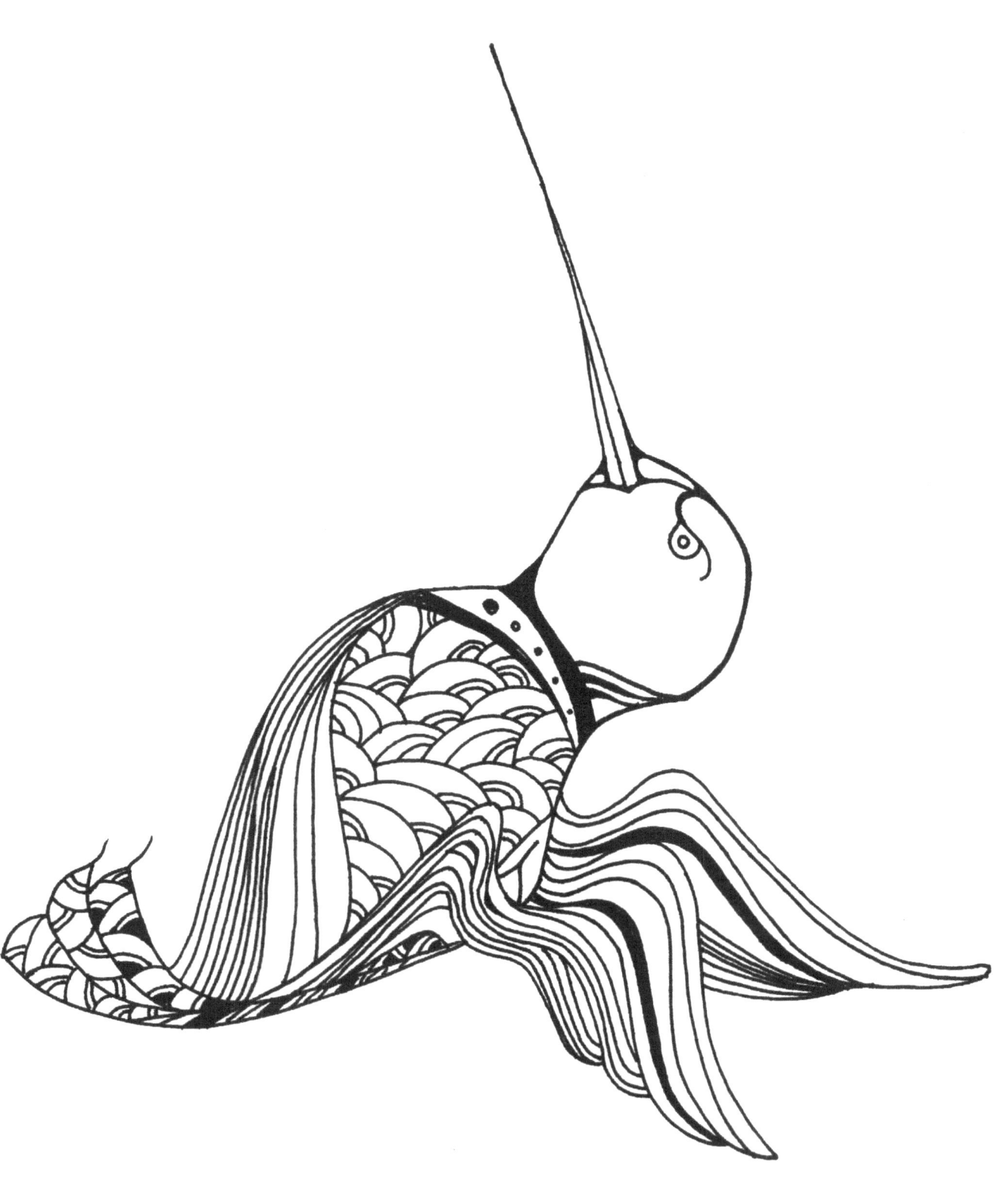

← ———————— 4

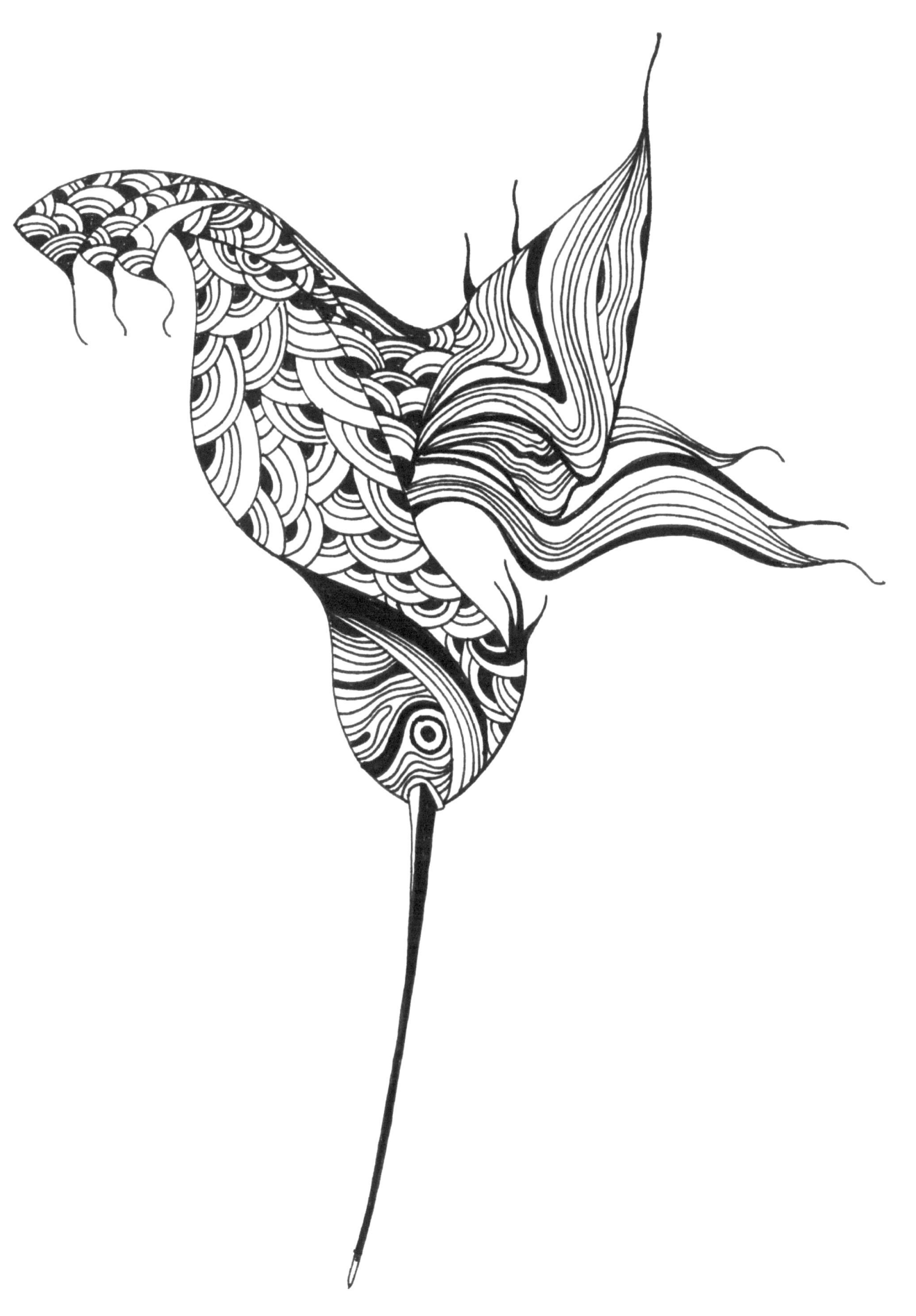

← ———————— 5

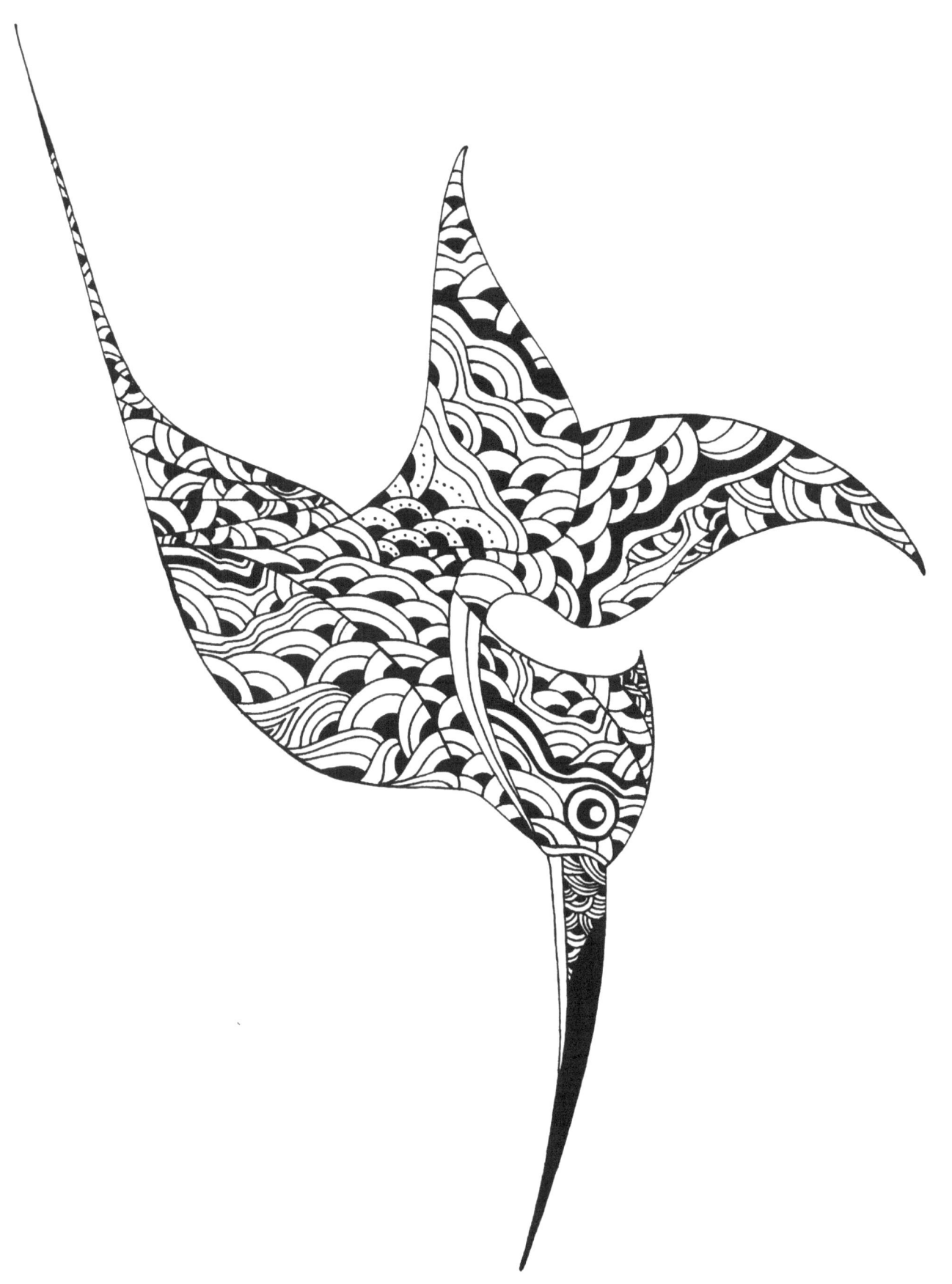

6

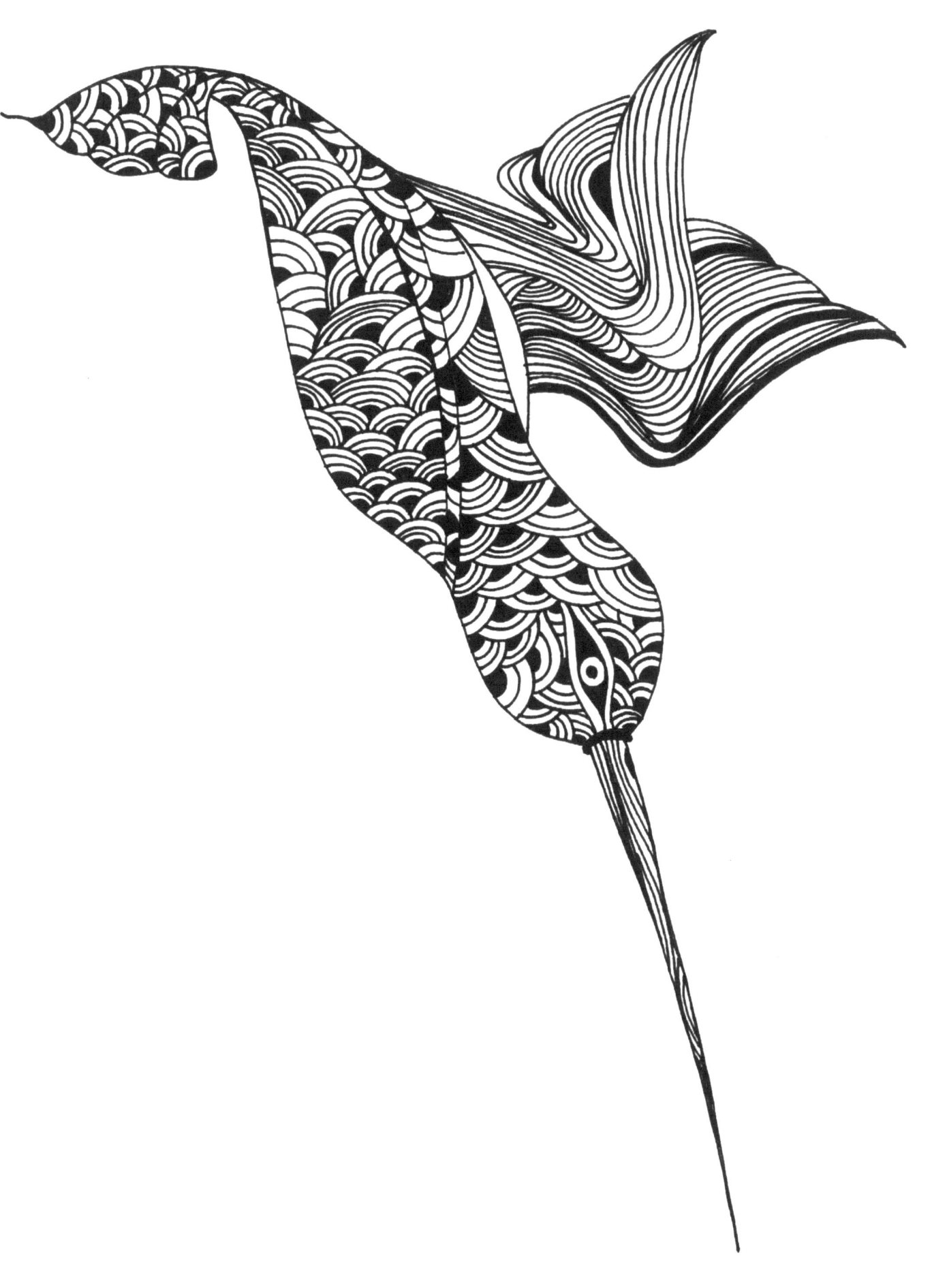

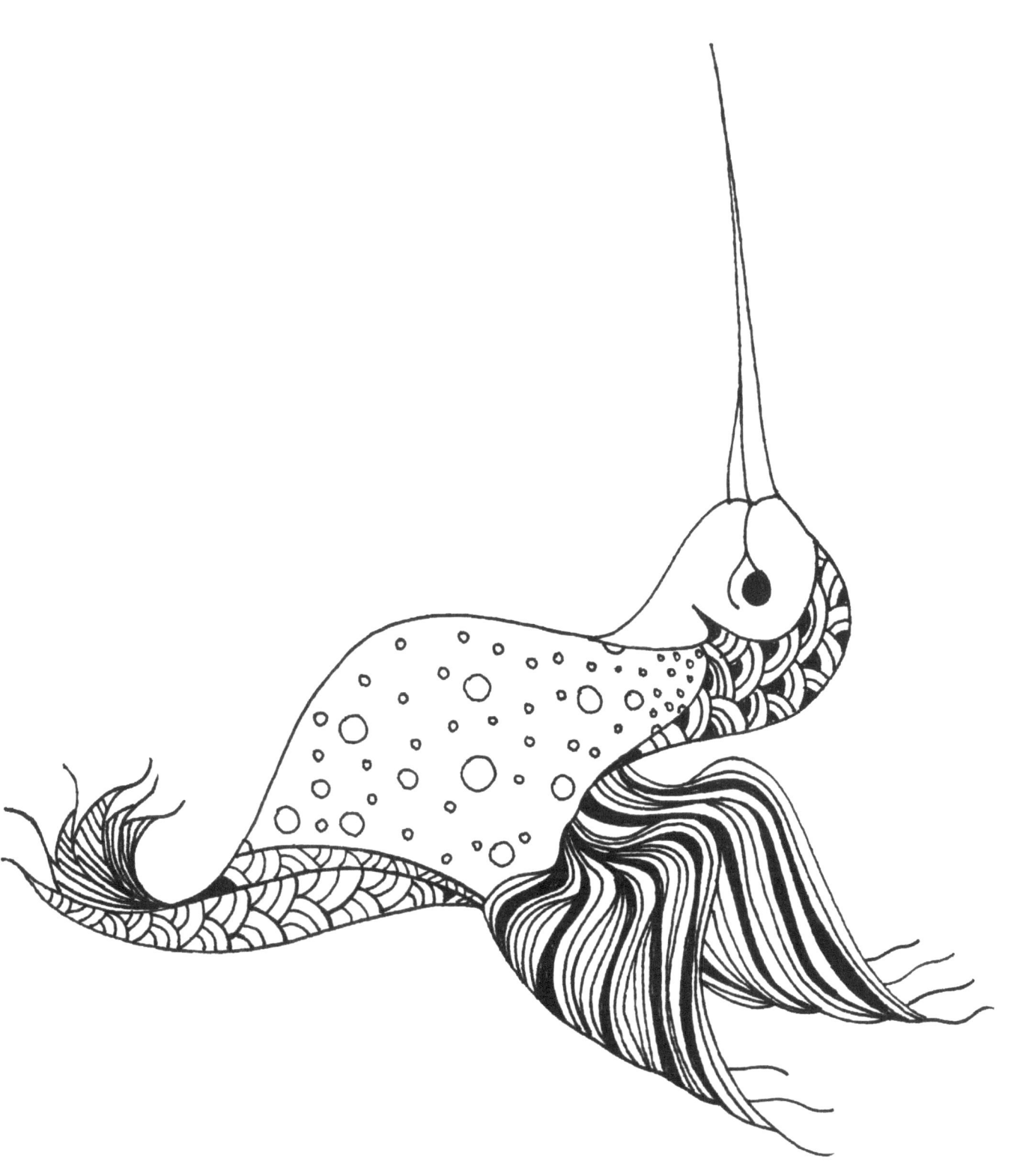

8

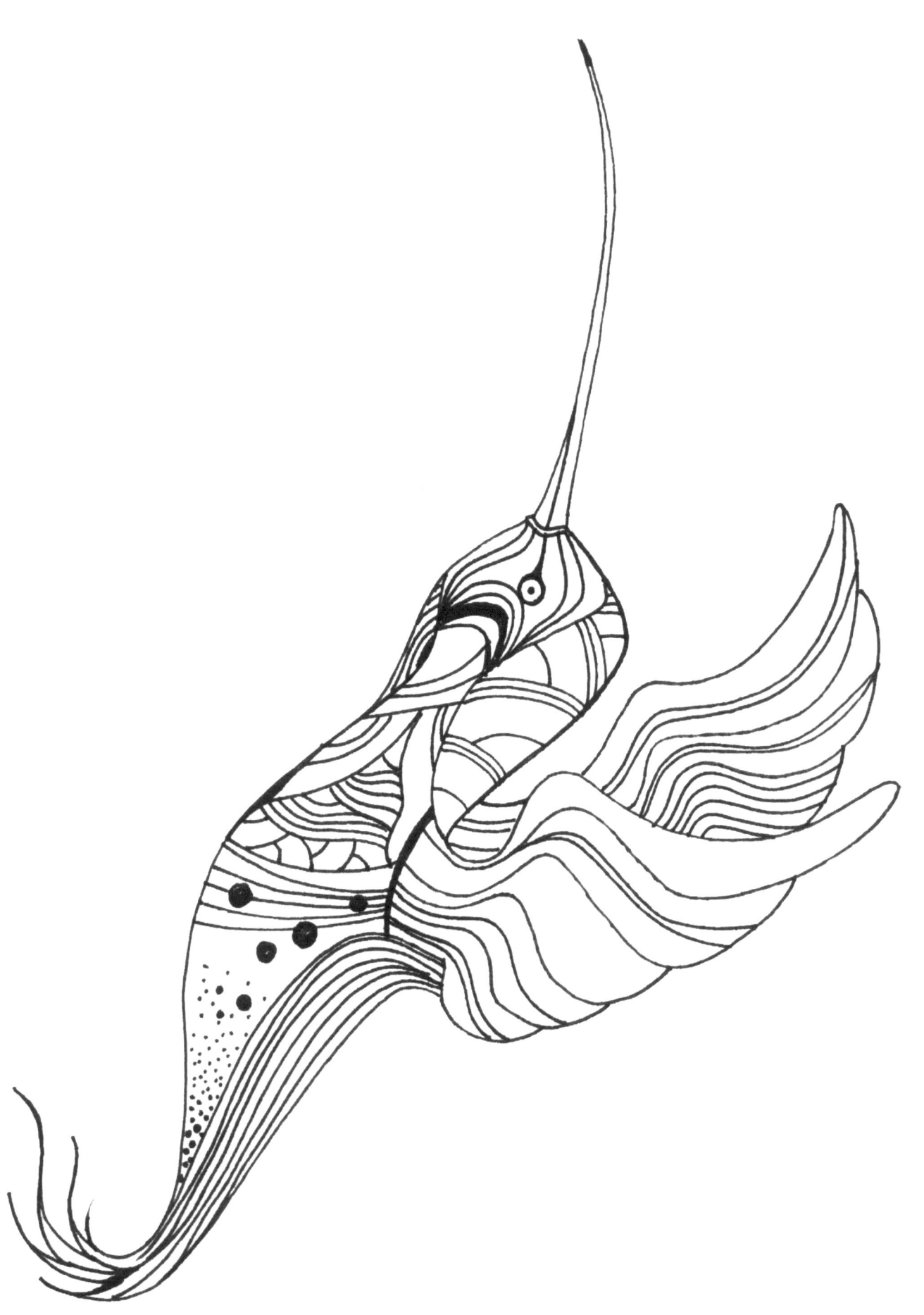

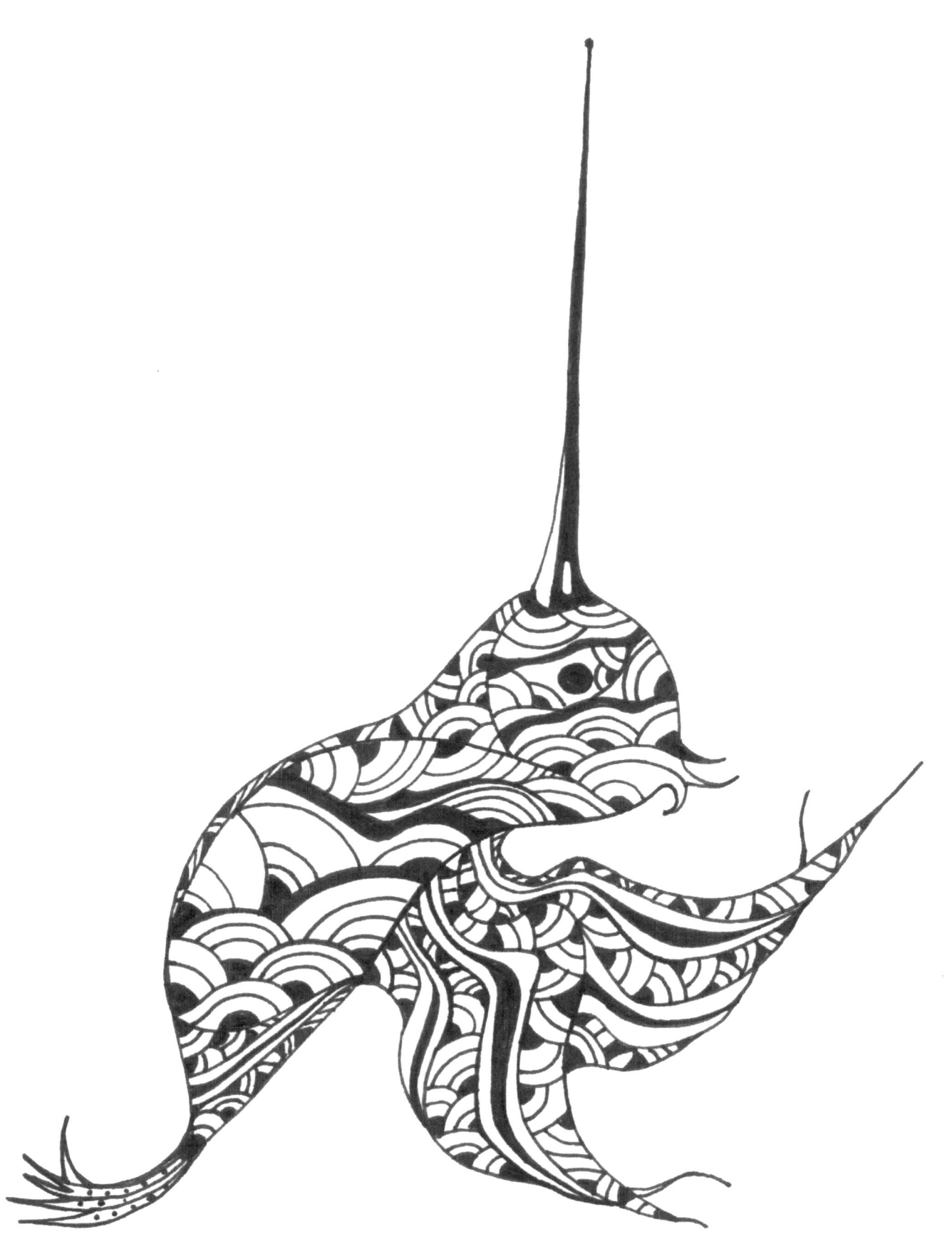

← ———— 10

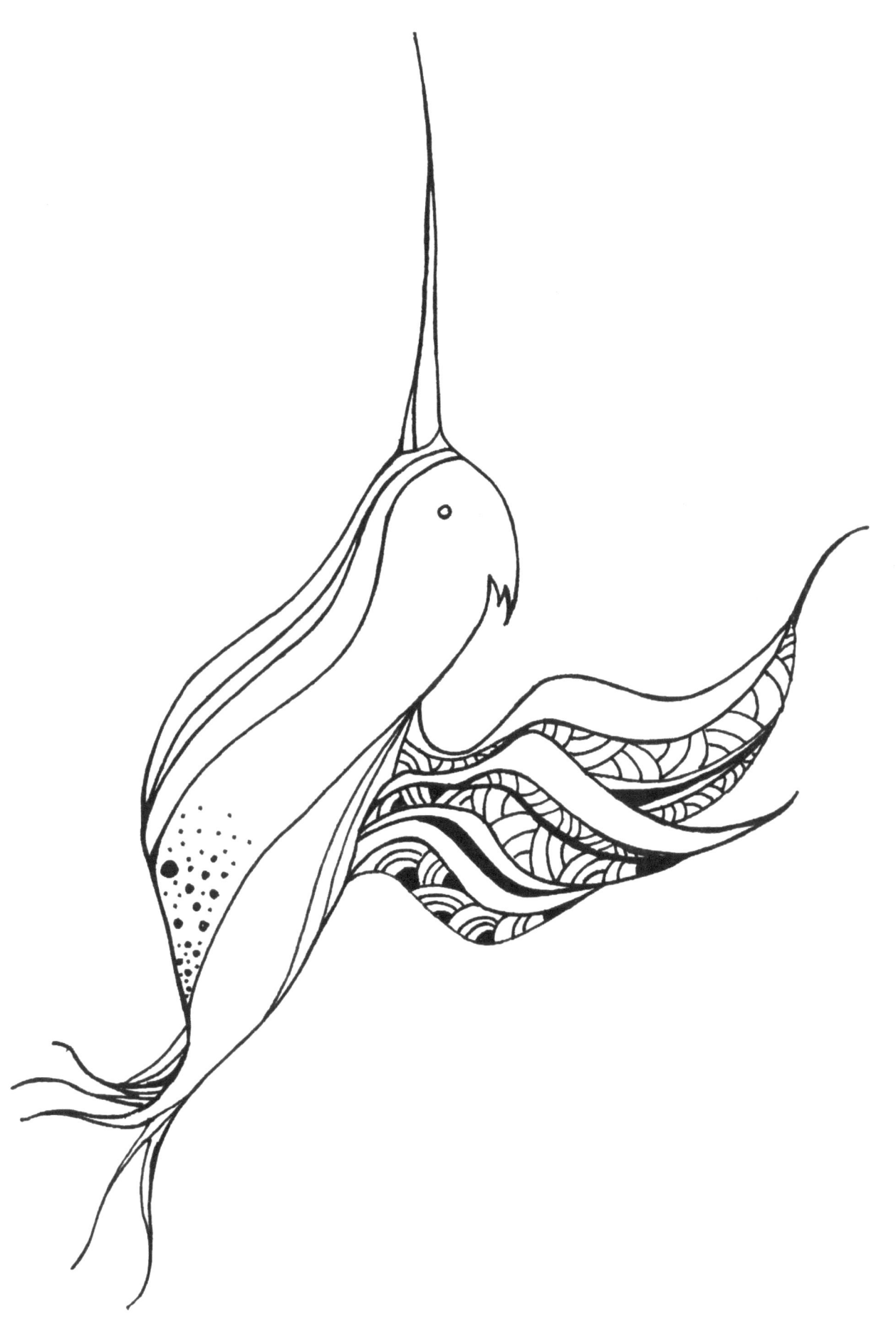

← ———— 11

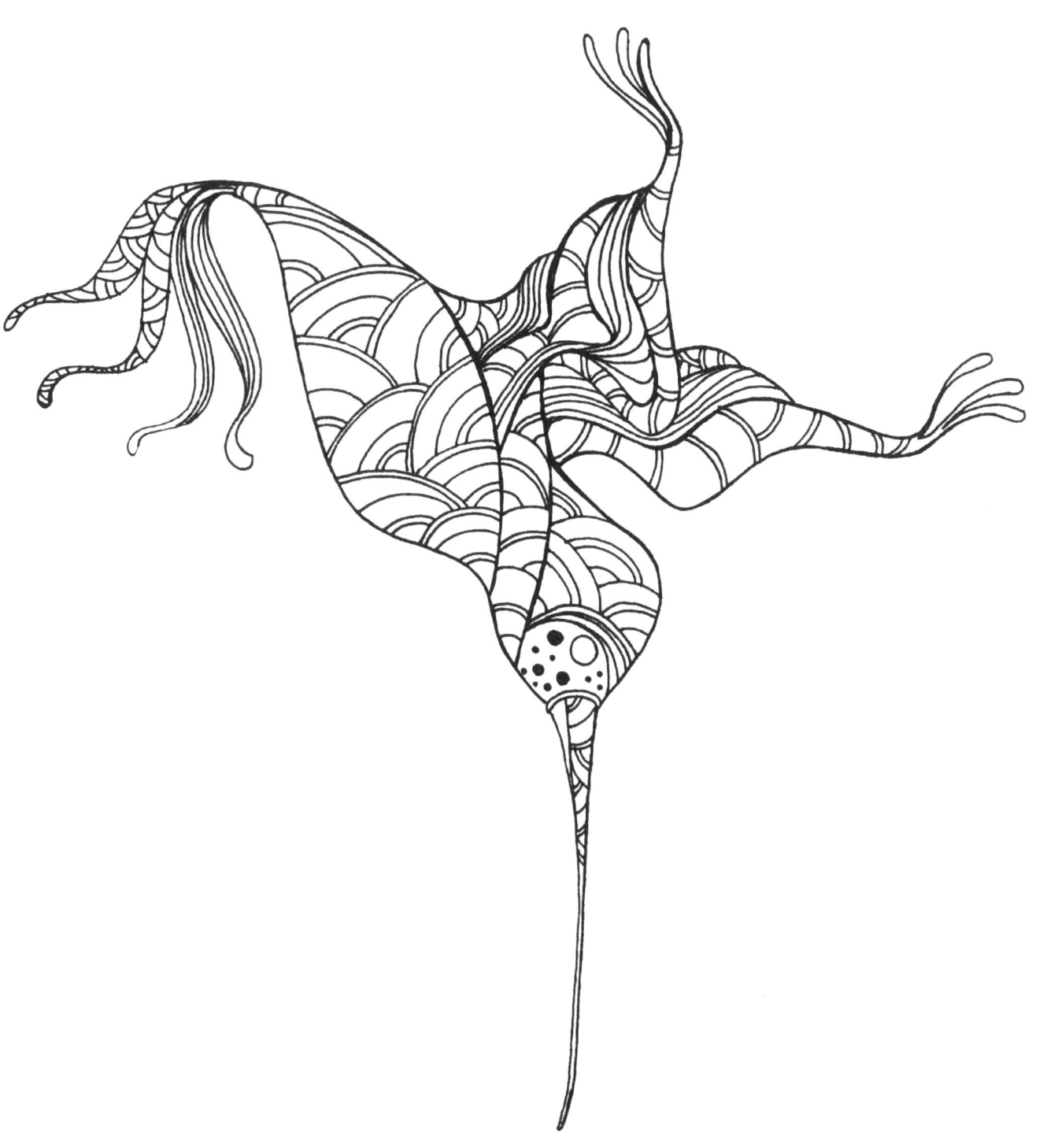

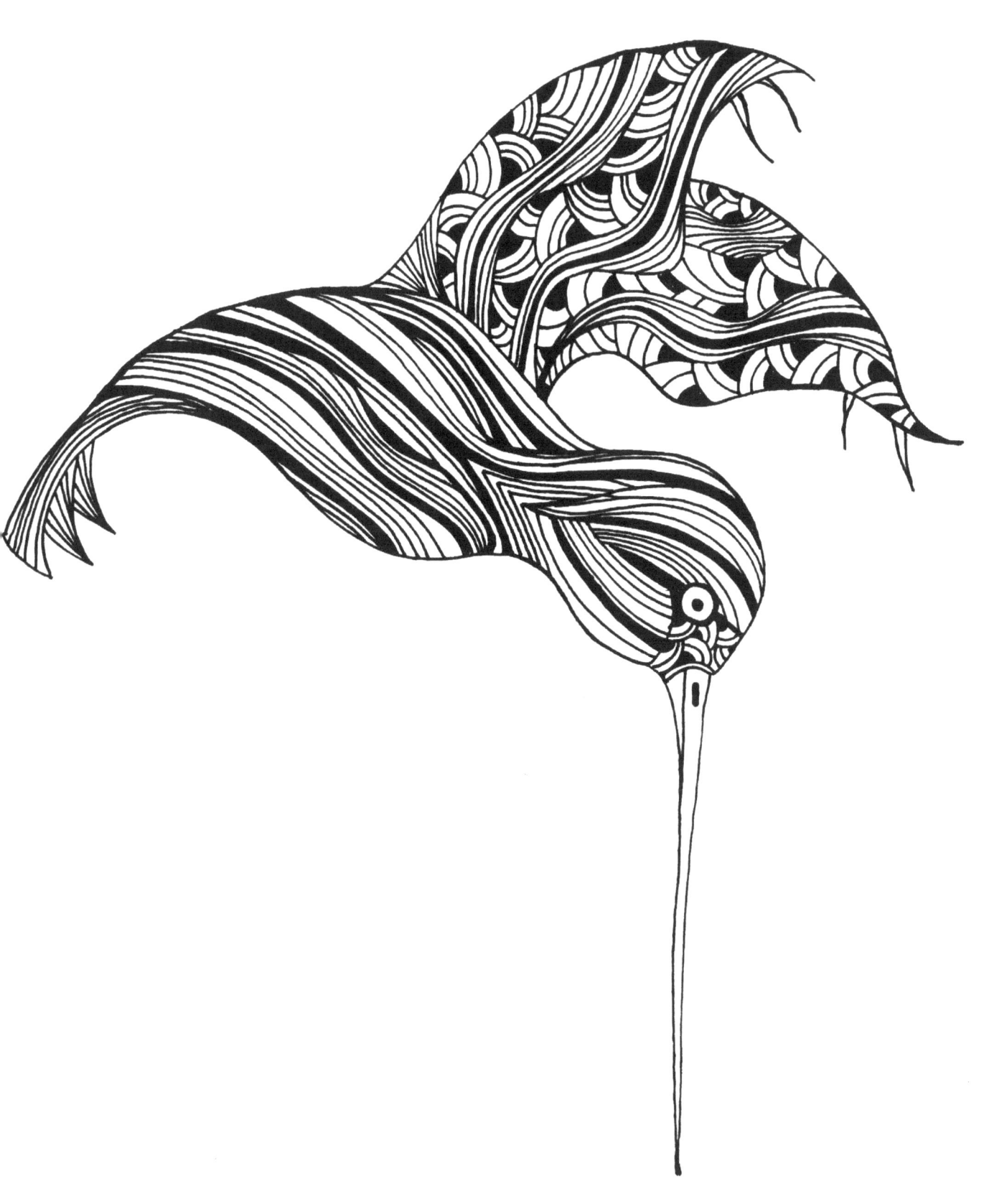

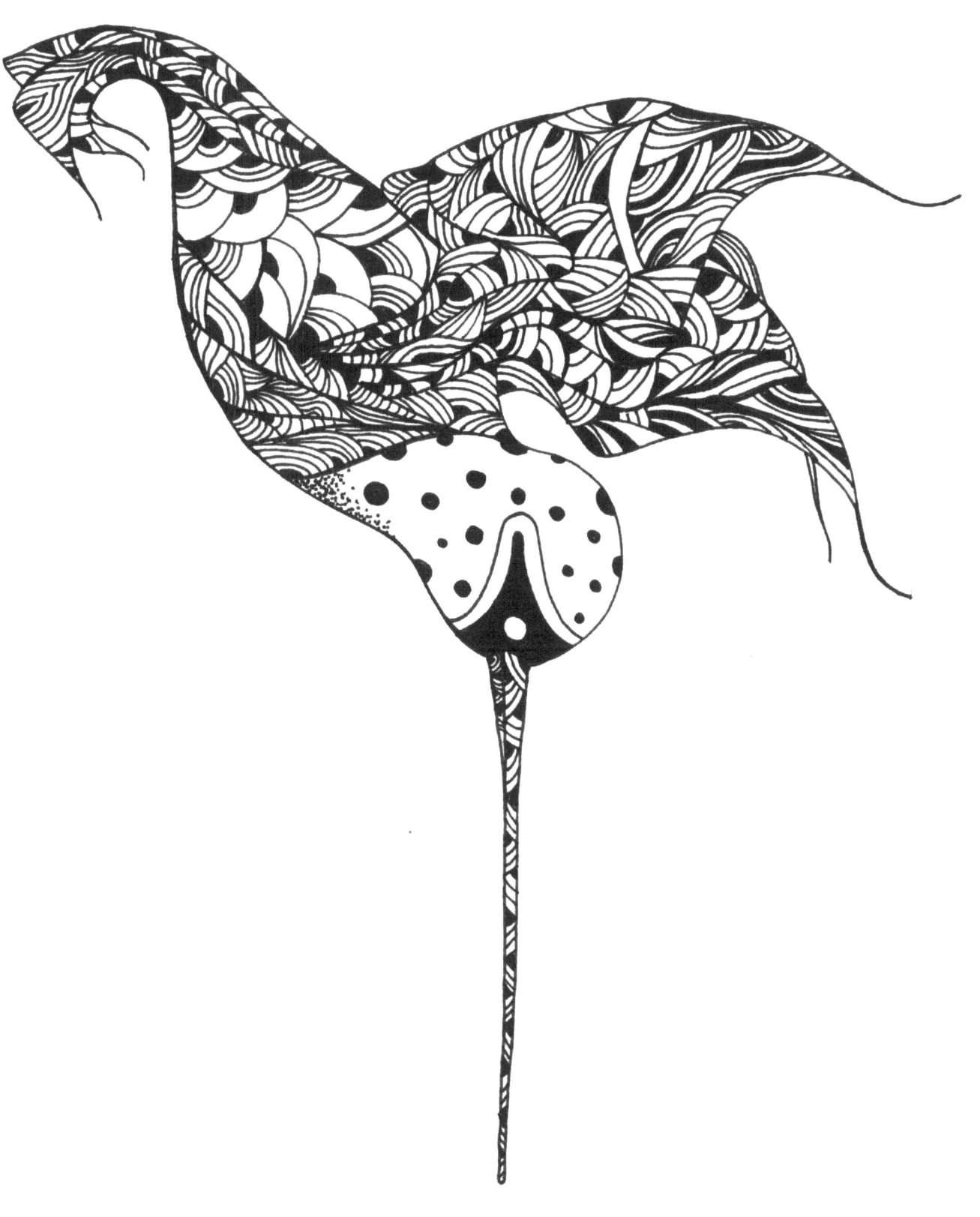

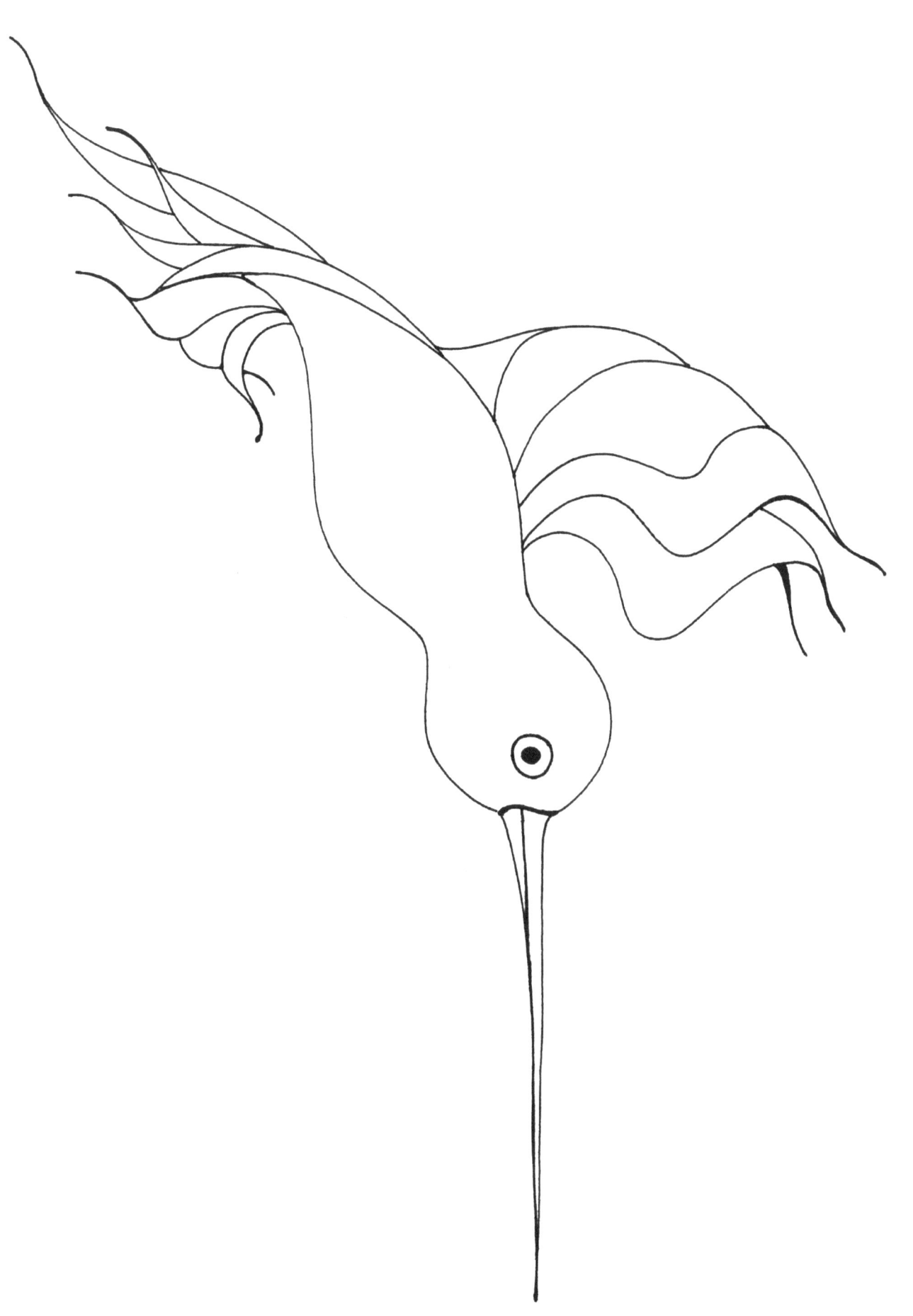

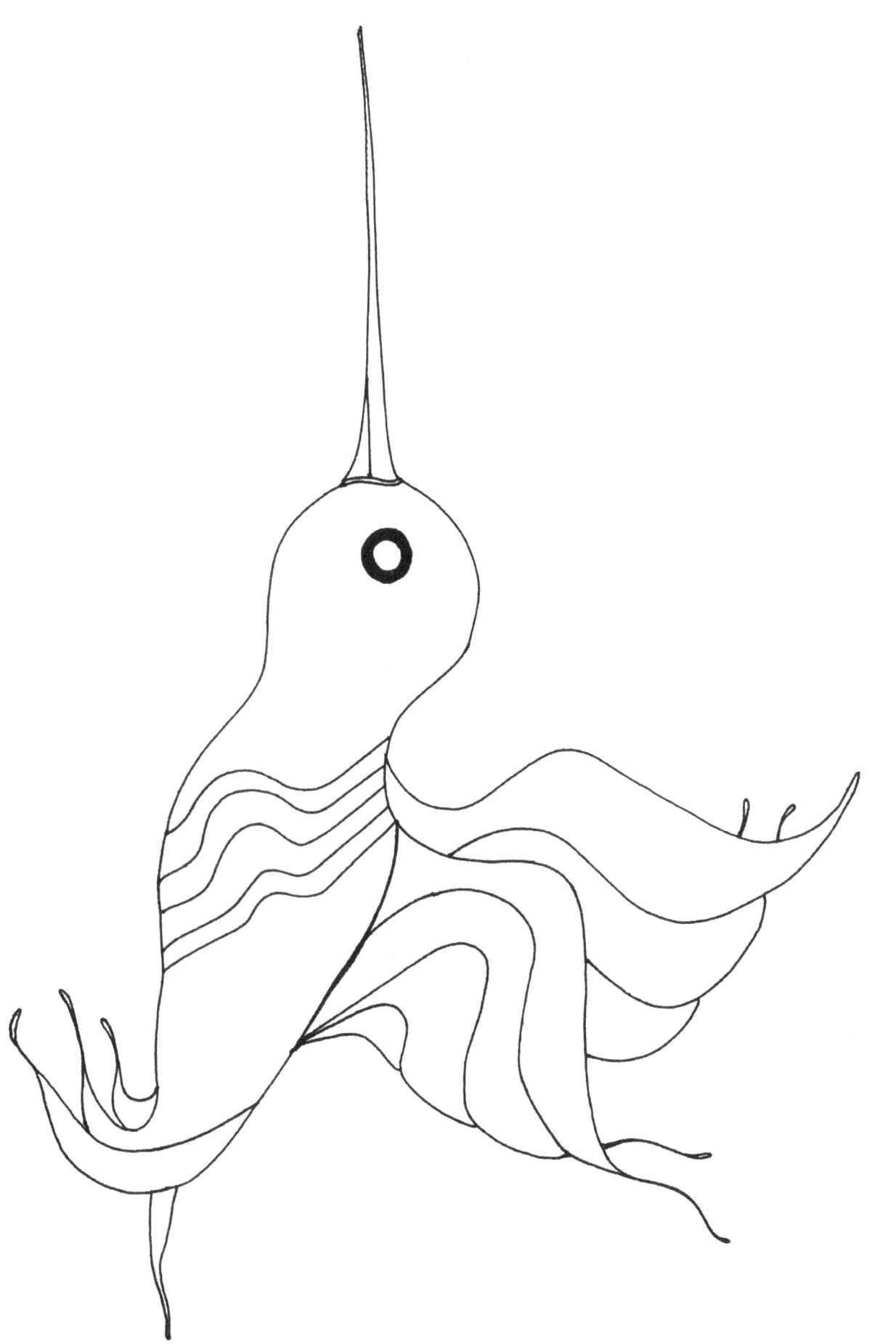

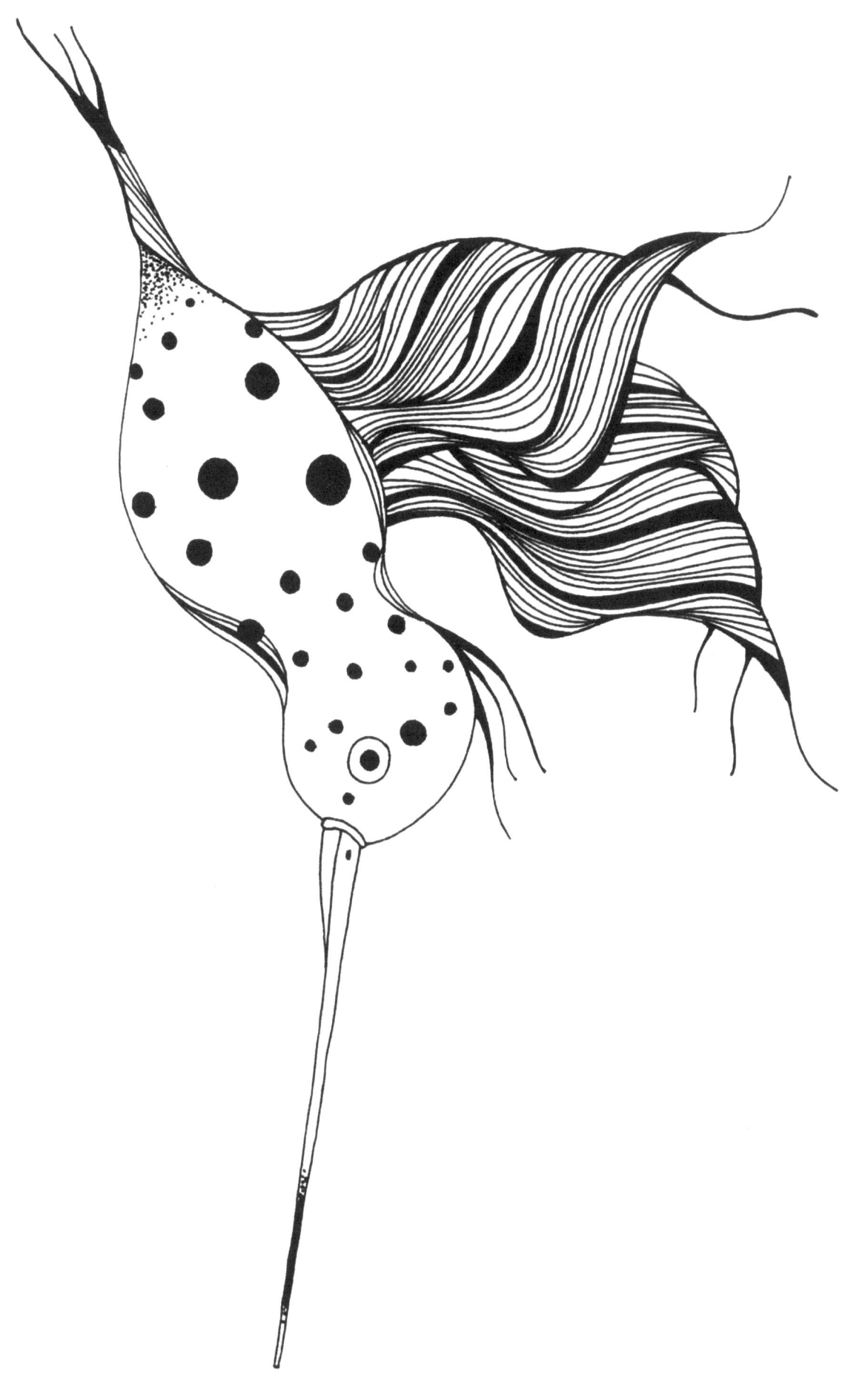

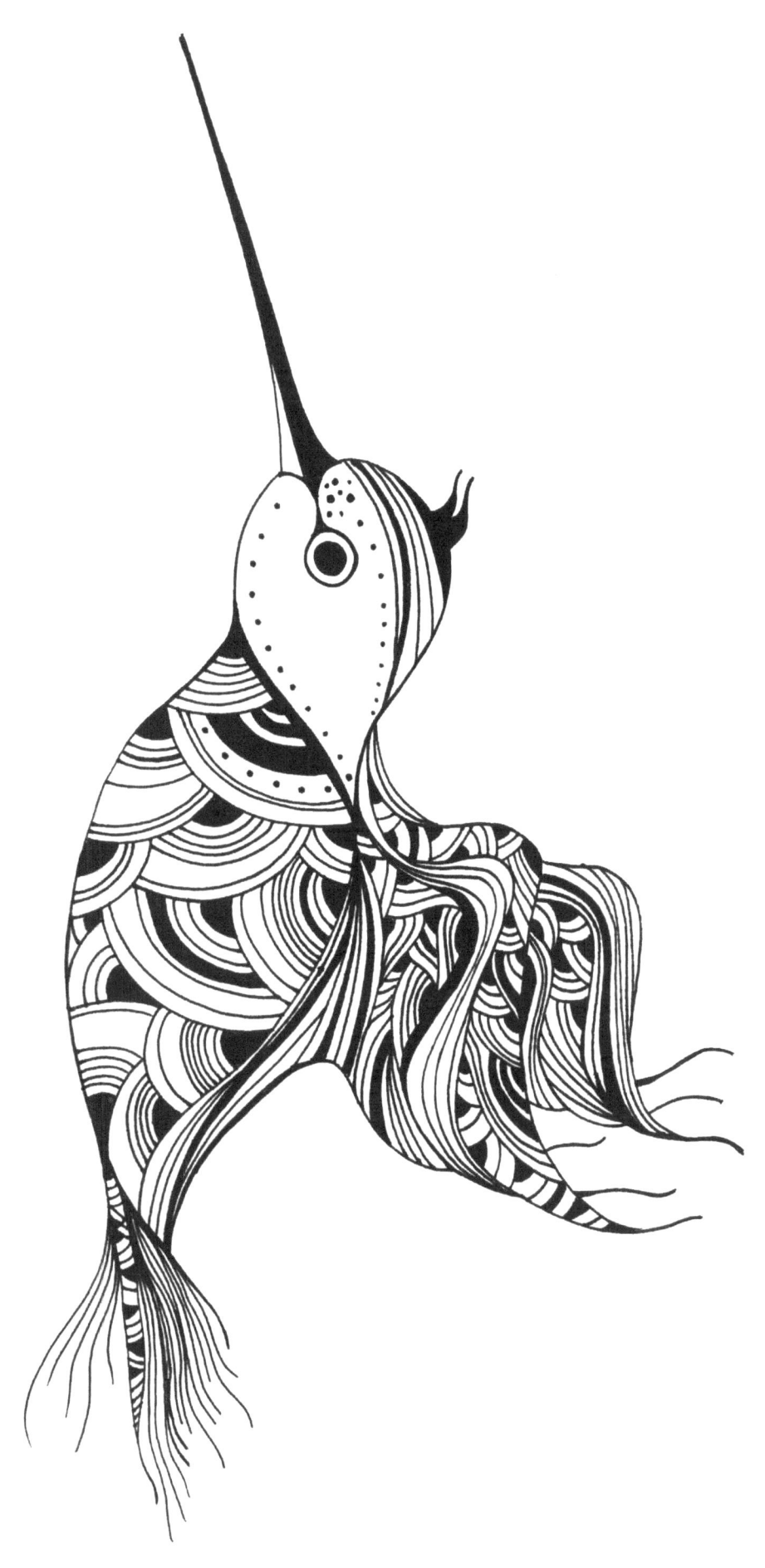

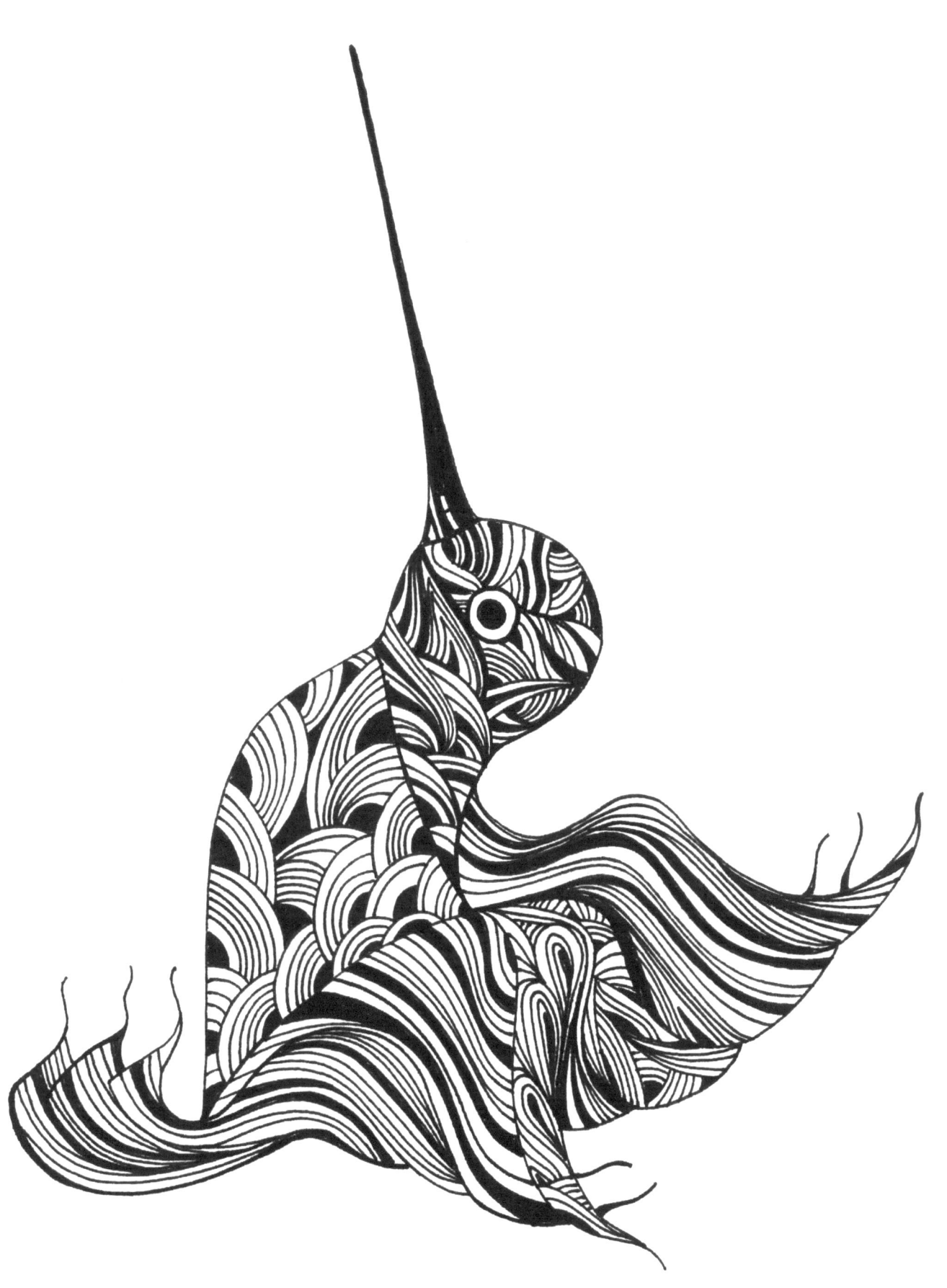

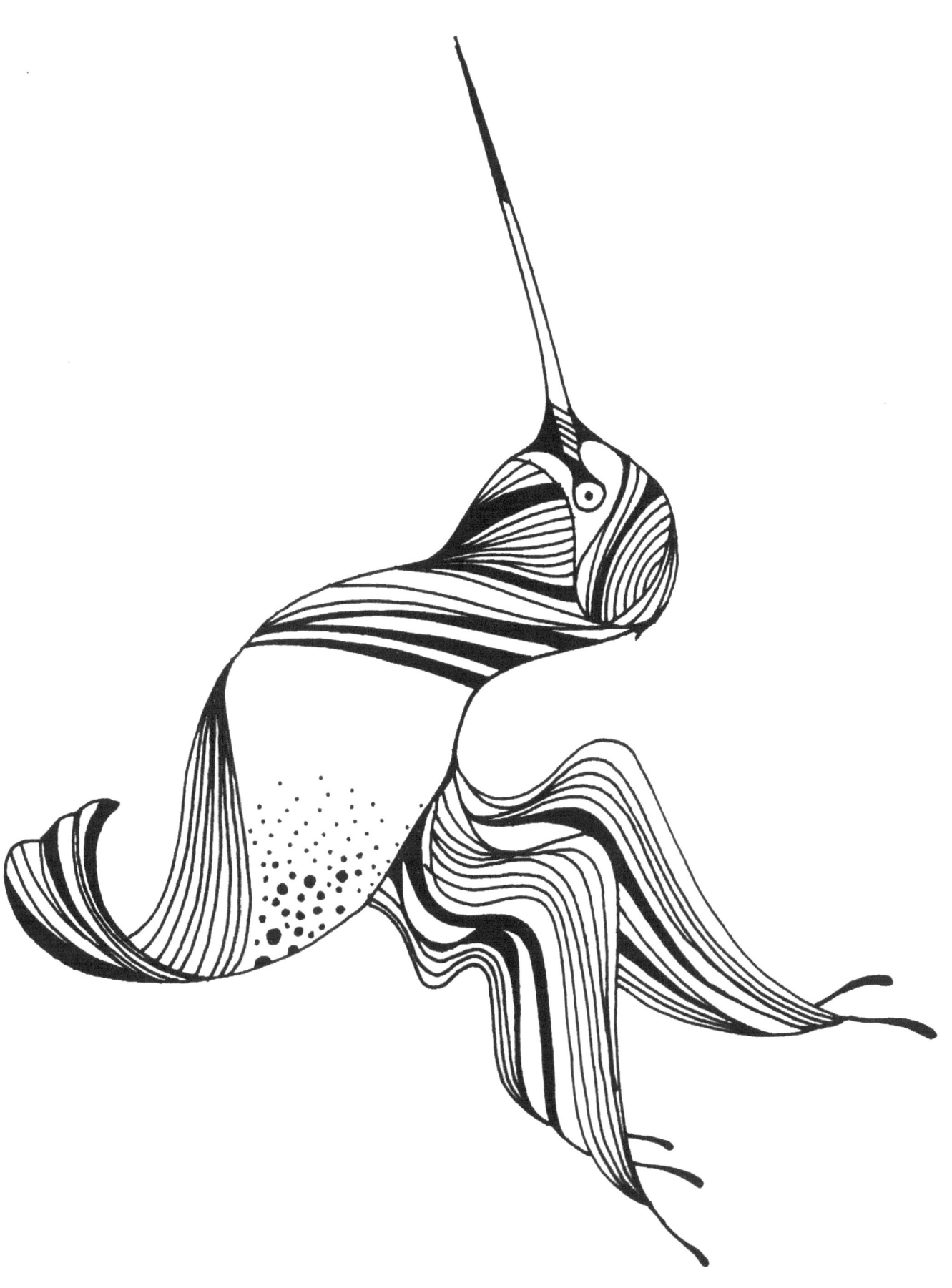

← ———— 20

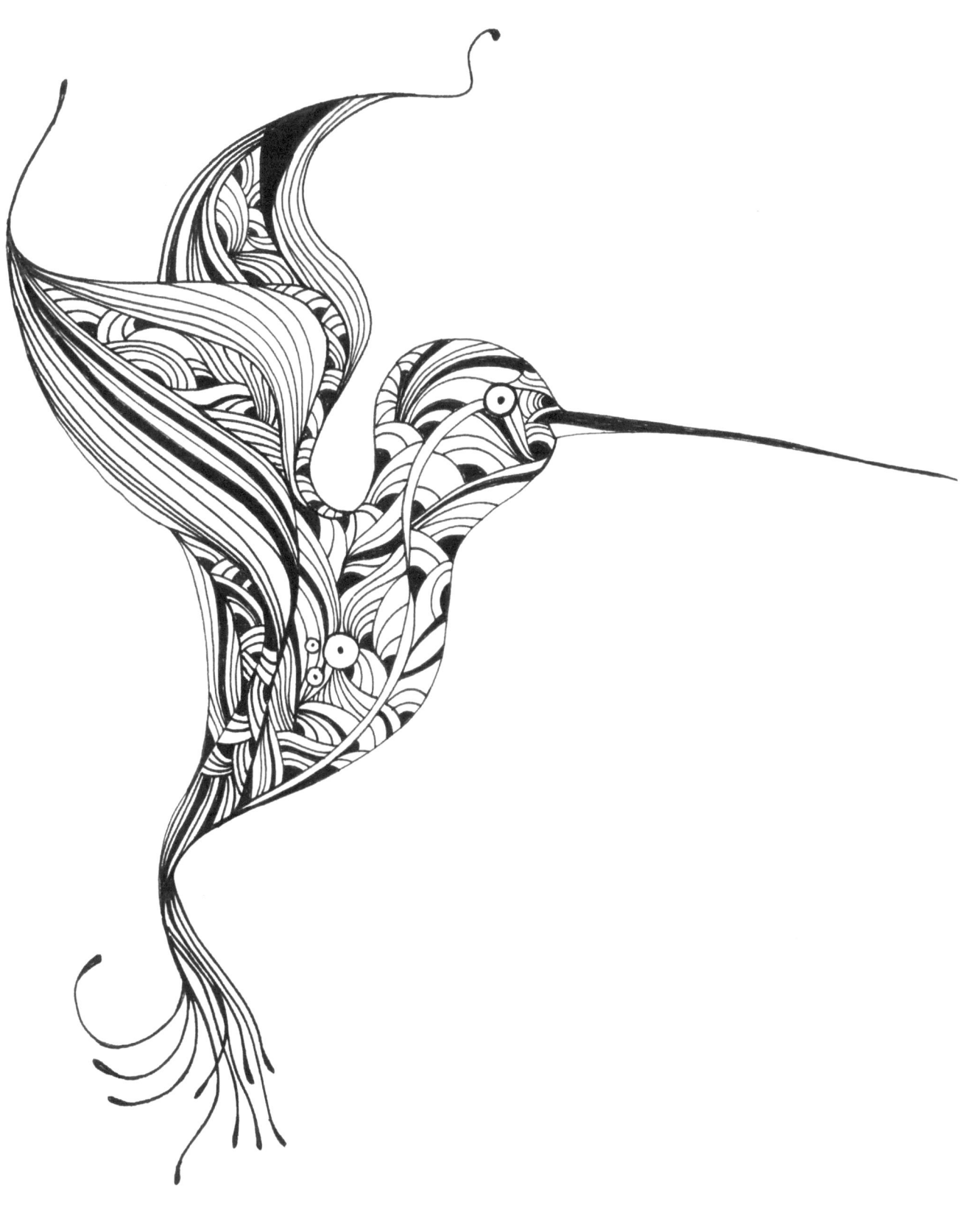

Here are other images from the rest of the series.
Collect all five volumes.

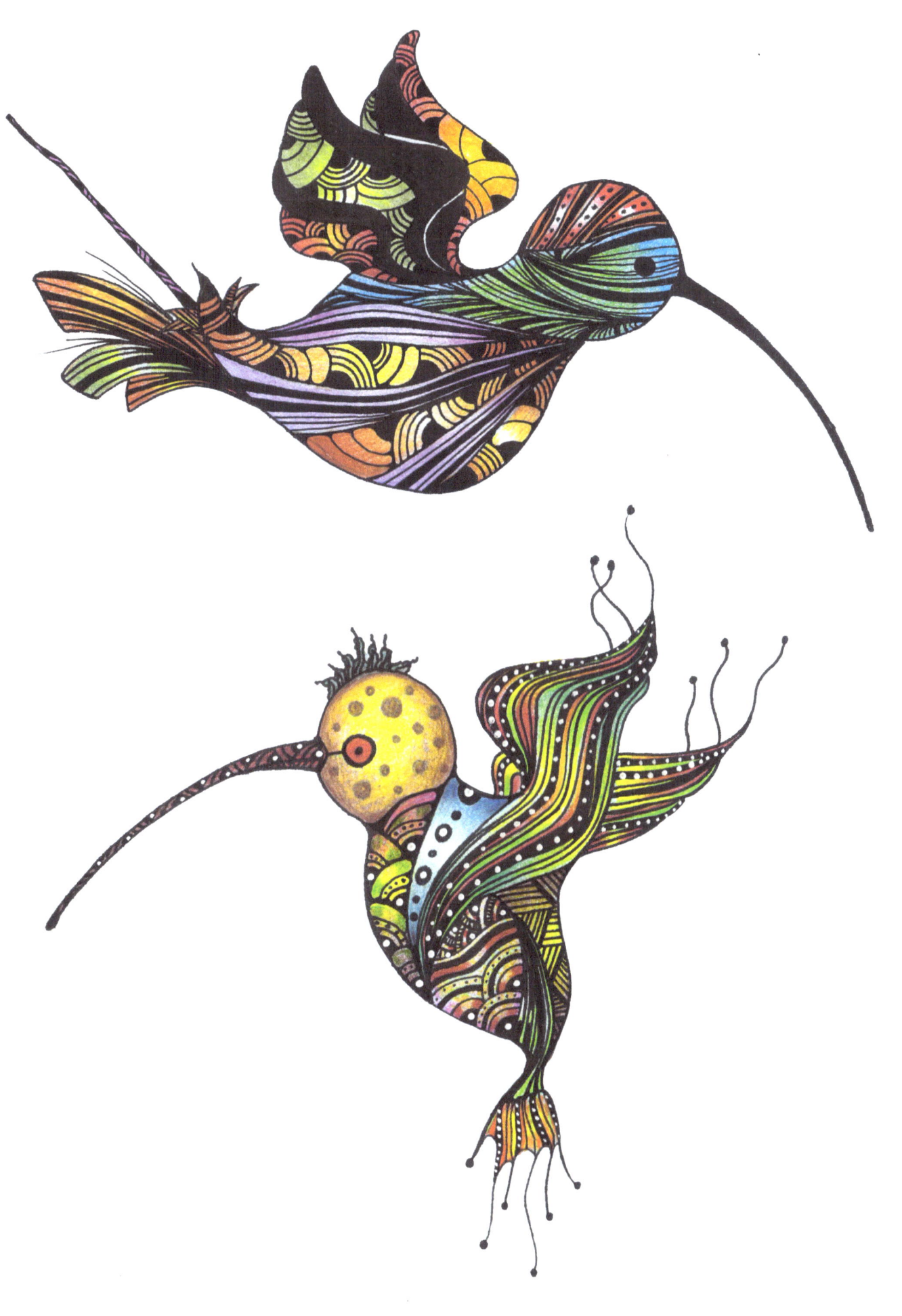

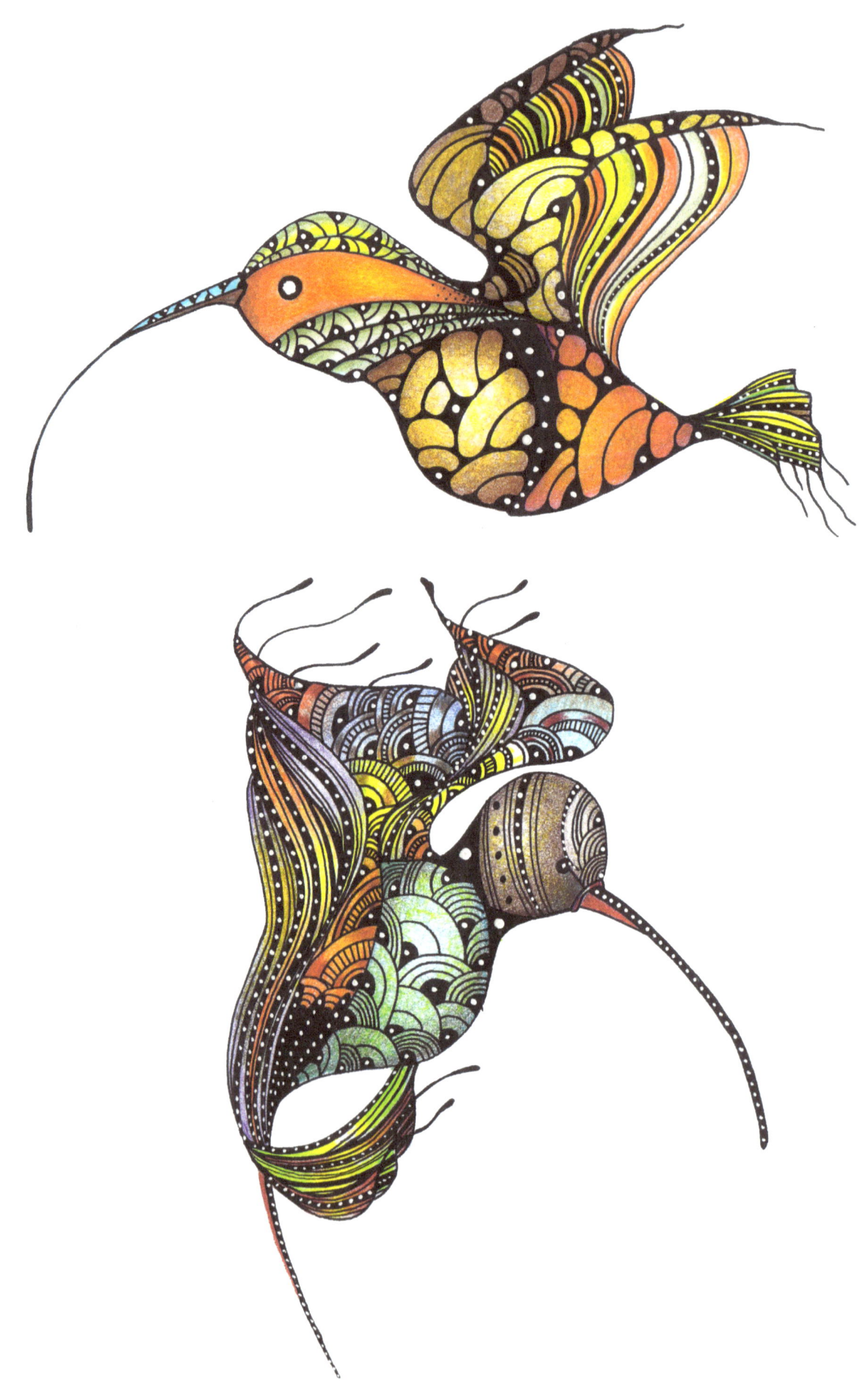

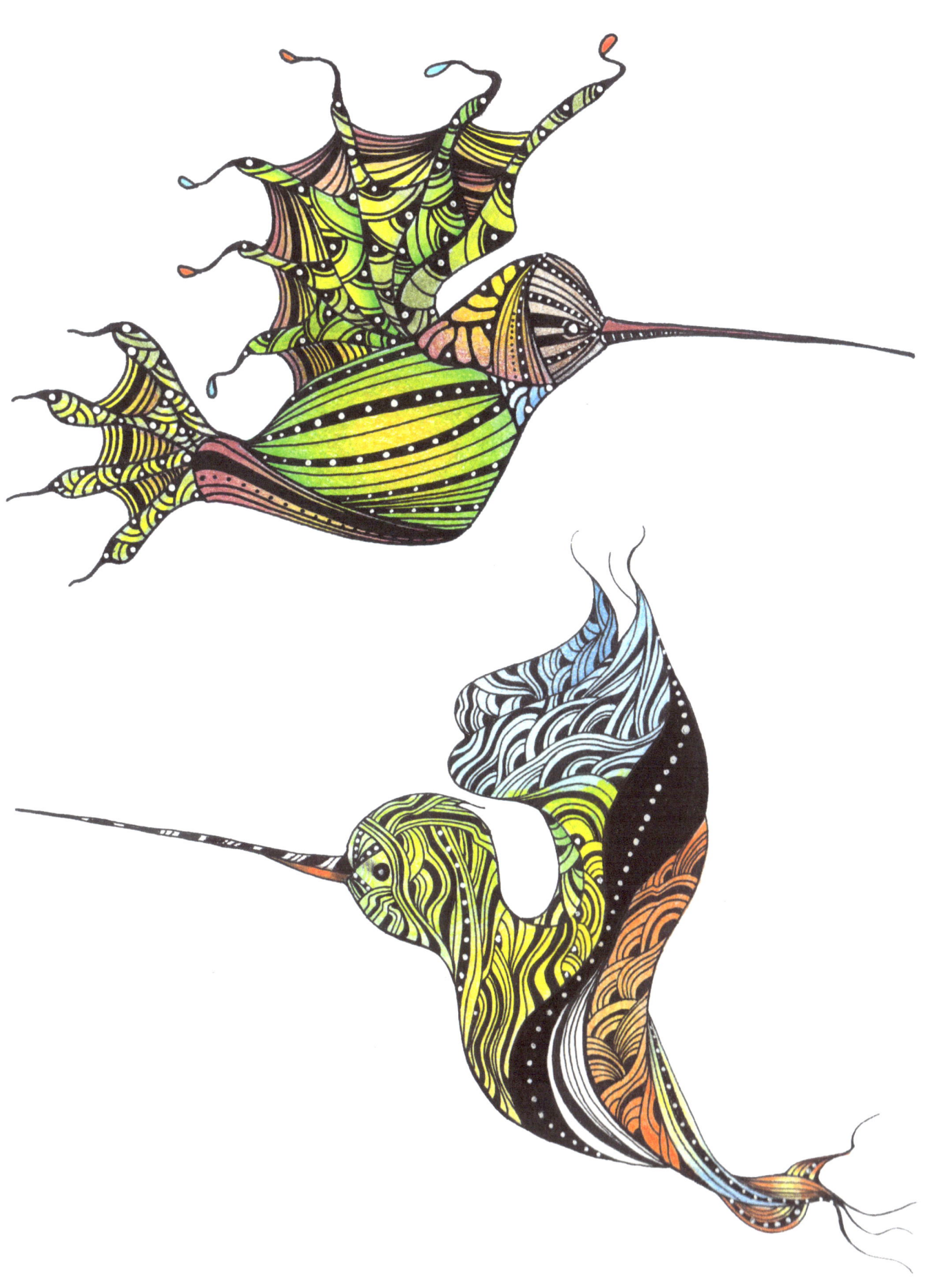

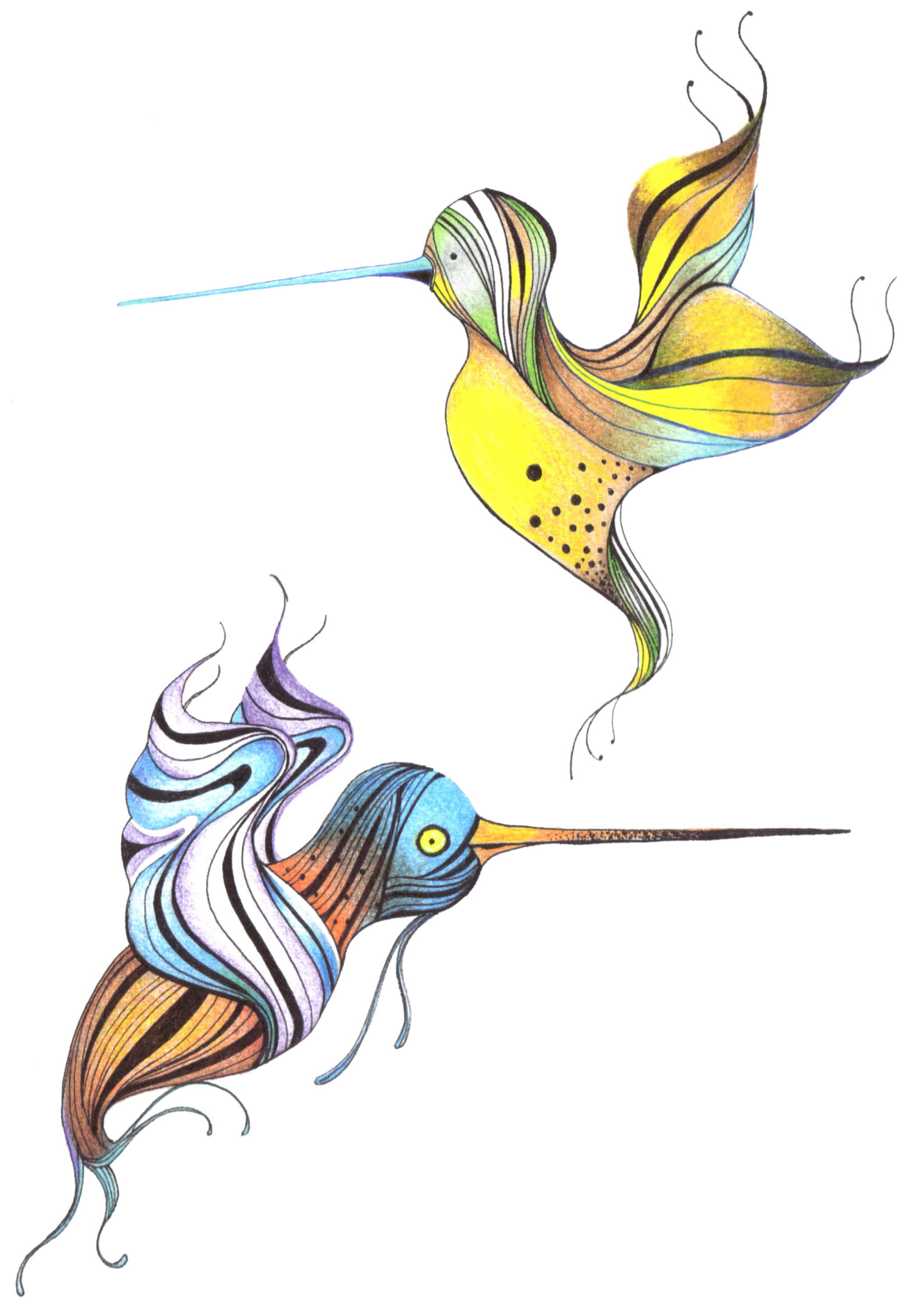

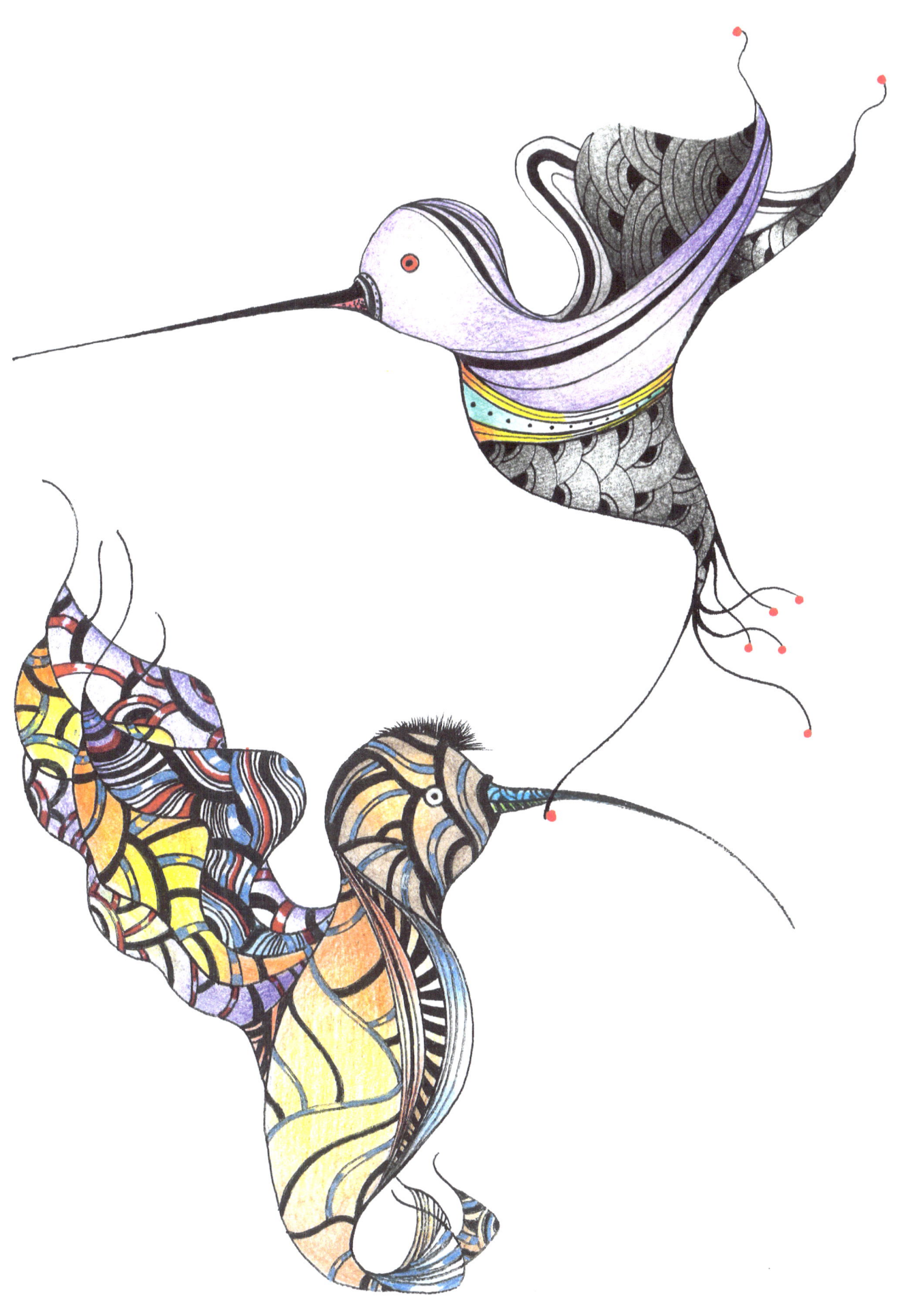

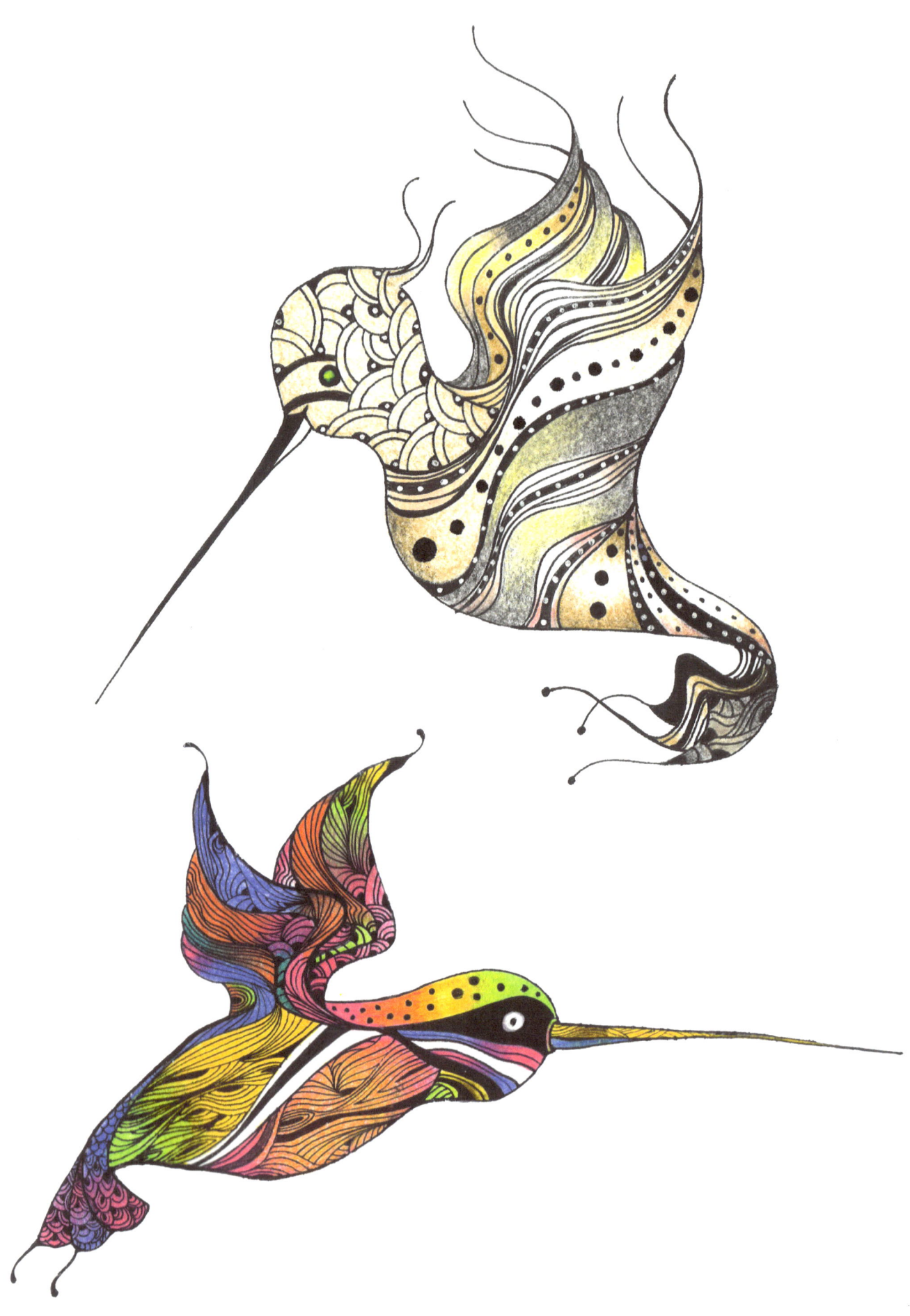

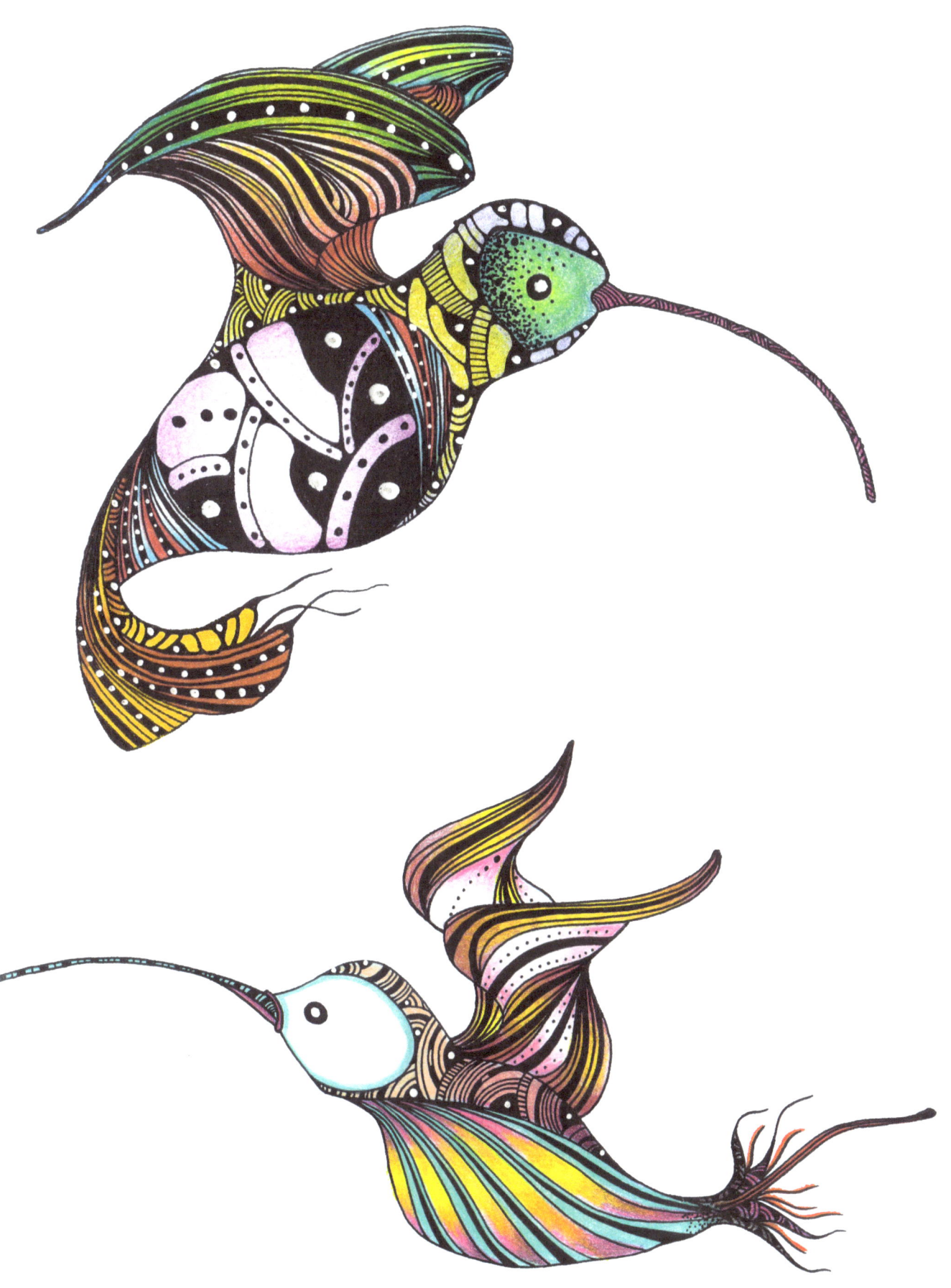

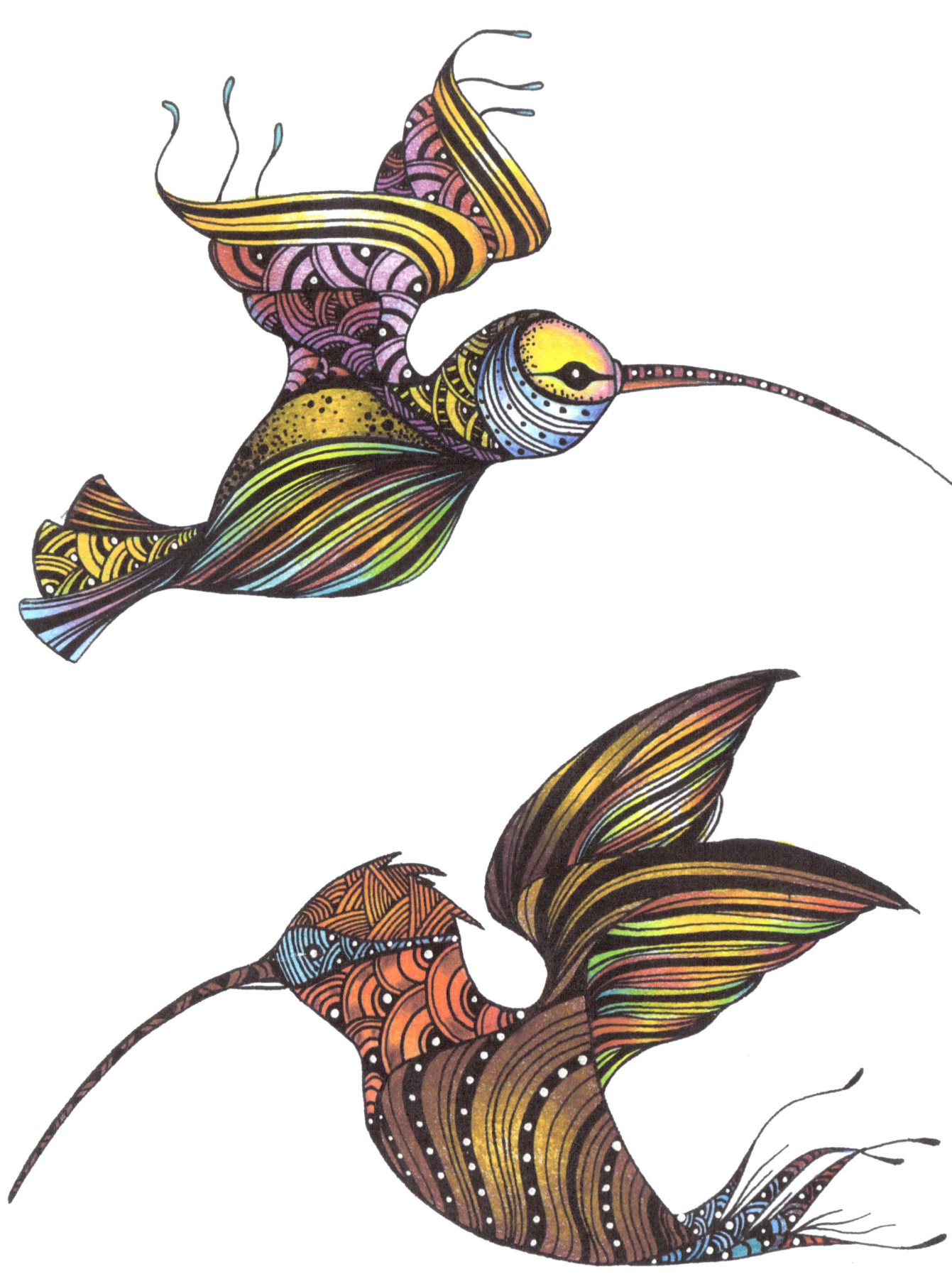

Color Bars

Use these bars to test your coloring medium and palette. Don't be afraid to try unique color combinations.

Color Bars

Use these bars to test your coloring medium and palette. Don't be afraid to try unique color combinations.

Color Bars

Use these bars to test your coloring medium and palette. Don't be afraid to try unique color combinations.

Color Bars

Use these bars to test your coloring medium and palette. Don't be afraid to try unique color combinations.

www.ingramcontent.com/pod-product-compliance
Lightning Source LLC
Chambersburg PA
CBHW050856180526
45159CB00007B/2691